COUNTERFEIT

COUNTERFEIT

Lies That Cover The Naked Truth

KATRINA SPIGNER

Brandol,
Walk Boldly on your
journey to uncovering! Keep
shimmering light and love!
I am grateful for our
friendship!
Love 2014

Published by breathe N.O.W. Publishers
Cover Design by Langley Burch Consulting
Edited by Dr. Kristie Searcy, Class "A" Editing

All Scripture quotations are taken from the Holy Bible, New King James Version (NKJV ®), copyright 1979, 1980, 1982, Thomas Nelson, Inc. Publishers. THE HOLY BIBLE, NEW INTERNATIONAL VERSION®, NIV® Copyright © 1973, 1978, 1984, 2011 by Biblica, Inc.® Used by permission. All rights reserved worldwide. *The Message.* Copyright © 1993, 1994, 1995, 1996, 2000, 2001, 2002. Used by permission of NavPress Publishing Group.

ISBN: 978-1-60047-264-0

Printed in the United States of America

0   1   2   3   4   5   6

CONTENTS

FOREWORD

For the majority of us, our lives have been "shaped" by our experiences, culture, religion, and tradition. We answered the "call" of God and now find ourselves caught between two dynamics. They include our hidden issues and Christian lifestyle expectations. Even though the bridge between these dynamics is the word of God, we find ourselves ignoring or skipping the necessary process of transformation for the "look" of freedom (2 Peter 1: 2-10).

In our innocent attempts to fit in and be accepted, we create "pressure" within ourselves to reach some "level" of Christianity. In turn we conform our lives to the routine of Christian Living, instead of taking the time to transform our lives with the "bridge of truth". We miss the empowerment that comes with going through the process regarding our issues which develops relationship and maturity in our covenant with God (Romans 8:18).

This process develops our "new" identity which is "shaped" by the transformational process of allowing truth to deal with our issues…unashamed. God is concerned about us. He understands that we have issues and He desires us to LIVE in FREEDOM not PRETEND we are Free.

So, Katrina has become the voice and heart of God expressed in this season, to give us permission to deal with the issues in our lives that we have hidden by asking three poignant questions. "Where Are You?" "Who Told You That You Were Naked?" "What Is This You Have Done?" Allow her transparency through this work to be a support, guide, path and safe place to explore and cross your bridge to true FREEDOM. It is time.

-Stephanie M. Kirkland,
Author of *The Eve Dilemma*

This Part of the Book Is Important Too...

Why the Introduction?

I begin this book with a portion of my life's story because it is important for you to know that I do not approach this book's content as the *expert*, but rather as the *experienced*. Therefore, I want to set the stage for our journey together through the pages of what is to come. I want to establish with you a sense of "realness" – a place of personal vulnerability and transparency - Authenticity. I want to give you a glimpse into my life's experiences so that you will not feel alone as I challenge you to look deeply into your own.

By allowing you access into the places in my life where I have experienced the thrill of victory and the agony of defeat, my hope is that you will tap into the courage to open your own doors and peer directly into the hidden compartments of your life – the good, the very good, the bad, the very bad, and the ugly – the very ugly.

As you enter in, no matter what you find, my hope is that you will be inspired to grab the courage you need to emerge from the shadows of your own deep dark places that have held you captive and kept you from stepping into the light. I hope you hear the voice of courage that summons you out of hiding when hiding would be the easiest thing to do. I hope you will allow courage to be the compass on a path that has never been traveled before – while pointing you toward freedom with every step.

As you come face-to-face with your own truths, I hope you allow courage to be the arms that embrace you while everything else in you trembles as you make your way to the invaluable prize of authenticity. It is my hope that you will desperately, with all your might, go after the power on the inside of you to tell your own authentic story – even if you are only telling your story to yourself.

Why Tell Our Stories?

Our stories matter. I am a firm believer that we are the sum total of all of our experiences. We are a conglomeration of each integral part of our past, every orchestration of our present, and all of the potential and hope for our future – we are all of those things – housed in one wonderfully created dwelling place, handcrafted by God.

We are his creation, sculpted in his image – a reflection of his likeness. We are his plan in action. We are his perfectly imperfect perfections – a true illustration of his Grace. We are flawed. We are scarred. We are bruised.

We have pieces. And yet, in him – we are whole. We are his intention – designed with his guaranteed promises attached. We are the embodiment of his goodness and mercy – encapsulated by his love.

We are an ever-evolving book, written by him, the author and finisher of our faith. We are held in his hands. We are complete in his heart. We are covered in his embrace. We are never forgotten because we occupy space in his mind. We are his delight. We are safe in him. Therefore, we can place our realities at his feet. We are never without his presence. We are never alone on our journey. We are his in spite of. We are his because of. We are his in the midst of.

However, life brings with it many opportunities for us to *not* know, or for us to forget, or for us to struggle with, or for us to ignore, or for us not to fully understand, or for us to question the truth of who we were created to be. Therefore, I chose to write about my own journey so that we might walk together as you set out on your own journey to answer the question life's been asking you.

Why Is This Book Necessary?

During my training to become a certified personal and executive coach, I was taught very early on that an effective coach has the ability to skillfully ask powerful questions that entice a person to go deep inside themselves to the core of who they are in an effort to find answers that come from a place only known by them. These powerful questions call us to search for responses that come from our truest and most authentic selves. In surgical like fashion, these questions cut through the superficial layers of our lives and probe into areas that house our own answers – answers we will never find until the right questions are asked. These powerful questions are the ones that invite us to explore our heart and soul in an effort to get to what is real and what is true about the experiences of our lives.

In the spirit of coaching, this book serves as a challenge to you to answer three of the most powerful coaching questions ever asked by the Coach of the Universe – God. This book is a response to the struggles we face with trying to live authentically. The book was written to serve as an up-close and personal one-on-one, face-to-face, intimate coaching session held in the privacy of your own world. Finally, this book was written to provide you with an opportunity for you to meet and get to know the most amazingly wonderful, exceptionally phenomenal, and uniquely distinguished person you will ever encounter – Your Authentic Self.

For Whom Was This Book Written?

First and foremost, this book was written for you. It was written for everyone who has had past struggles, who has present struggles, and who will have struggles in the future. The book was written to address your challenges with the ongoing warfare between living a life that is real versus a life that is counterfeit. This book was written to address the persistent restlessness and discontentment in your soul and the frustration you feel because you just cannot seem to "put your finger on" the real cause – but you always know it is there.

This book was written so that you could see firsthand the repercussions of illusionary living. This book was written so that you could recognize how the enemy of your soul seduces you into biting from the forbidden fruit of life while constantly providing you with sweet fruit-covered lies to entice you to keep eating.

This book was written for you to have a safe place to lay down the burden and weight of your secrets without fear of judgment, scrutiny, criticism, and shame. This book was written to give you permission to acknowledge to yourself areas of artificiality in your life. This book was written to give you a secure and non-threatening place to drop your guard. This book was written to expose guilt, condemnation, and embarrassment. Yet, it was written to inspire courage, spirit, and hope as you come out of hiding. This book was written for you to acknowledge your weaknesses, limitations, mistakes, transgressions, and failures. But, this book was also written for you to see the gift of living in the strength, power, lessons, triumphs, and victories that are yours through the God who loves you.

This book was written for you to honor, return to, and claim the person you were created to be before the foundation of the world and to discard any and everything in your life that is contrary to this truth. Yes, this book was written for you to pause to answer questions about your life – powerful questions – not to point you toward the perfect life, but rather to point you toward accepting that there is a perfect plan for your life.

How Should This Book Be Used?

This book is a tool to facilitate your journey into a deeper understanding of you – who you have been, who you are, and who you are becoming. It is a tool for assisting you in your quest to find answers – answers to the questions posed in these pages and that emerge in your life. This book is an accountability partner that beckons you to listen, to learn, and to live while challenging you to respond to what you are discovering about yourself and your life along the way.

This book is a personal identity checkpoint. It is an opportunity to release yourself to meet the real you. This book is a summons to authenticity – a call to the pure realness that abides at the core of your being. This book is a companion that accompanies you as you delve deep into the pockets of your soul to unearth nuggets that will change your life. This book is a catalyst for change. This book is a means to meaning. It is mirror in which you can see an image of who you are, of who you were created to be, and the transformation into the image of who are destined to become. This book is call to action – But greater than that – it is a call to hope.

Is it a Self-Help Book?

This is not a "self-help" book. The truth of the matter is that if we could help ourselves, we could calm the S.O.S. cries that come from our soul in the midst of life's greatest challenges and struggles. Yet, not even our intellect, skills, gifts, talents, nor abilities can bring us to sustaining peace. If we could help ourselves, there would be no need for answers because we would have no questions. This is not a self-help book because it is not designed to lead you down a path to believing that you can have the life you have always wanted in just a few easy-to-follow steps.

This book is not a "self-help" book. It is not intended to create an unrealistic approach to helping you to help yourself. It is not intended to establish an ideal against which you measure your success and later find yourself retreating because of the impossibility of meeting the established standard. In all honesty, if we could be consistently successful at helping ourselves, we would not have a need for help that comes from outside of our scope of human capacity. The reason this is not a "self-help" book is because if we could help ourselves, really help ourselves, there would not have been a need for Calvary.

What is the Author's Role in This Book?

As the author of this book, I want to offer you my hand. Why? Because you will be challenged. You will feel the insecurity and uncertainty of being asked to examine and dissect the realities of your life. However, as we walk together through the doors of those places in your life that rarely receive a visit; I want you to hear my encouragement in your ear as you brave the uncharted terrain of your own soul. As you face the dark, I want you to feel and know the light of hope. I want you know that you are not walking alone. Throughout this book, in every word, every sentence, every paragraph, every page, and in every chapter, as your personal coach, I am right there with you…out of the darkness and into the light.

In loving memory of my father, Minister Tryon Eichelberger, Jr. (1942-1999), whose legacy continues to cause me to dream.

INTRODUCTION

My Journey into Darkness (1997)…

Walk with me down the hall to the master bedroom. Now, come with me for a moment… I have something I want you to see and hear. Watch your step. Here we are. Go ahead, open the door and step inside. No, don't turn on the light. The darkness is a part of the plan. Okay, now stand here. Look over by the bed on the floor. I know it's hard to see because there is no light in the room. But look closely. Can you make out the image? Yes, that's me… Yes, really – the other me in another space in time, in another world very different than now, but yet, still me – the other me holding a gun. Listen to her as she tells her story:

How did I get here? How has my life gone so wrong? What happened to me? Where am I? Where is the woman I used to know? Where is the woman I used to be? With my body shaking from the rapid throbs and distressing sensations that consumed it as questions marched through my mind to a cadence of sorrow, I wondered. My t-shirt pulsated in the rhythm of my heart's pounding as if it was trying to beat its way free from the weakening vessel that held it hostage - thump thump...thump - thump thump...thump - was the tempo in my ear. With fast and shallow breaths, my soul languished from the unending pain, agony, and relentless misery engulfing it. My mind, my will, and my emotions gave way to the torment and fatigue that had weakened and cracked each part in places and rendered them dysfunctional.

A dualistic life – smiling on the outside while emotionally, mentally and spiritually deteriorating on the inside had taken its toll and depleted every resource I had – all in an attempt to keep sustaining a reality that was never really real at all.

An escalating heat filled the inner walls of my body, simmering, on its way to a complete boiling point. Yet, on the outside, a chill that brushed over me in wave-like forces of Nordic air enveloped my body. I was suffering. Yet, my suffering was not the result of physical illness or disease. No, the pain I was experiencing transcended the physical realm. It was pain that resided deep within the core of a place that could not be explained – a hidden place – a secret place.

This place had become a fortress, housing the hurts that "good Christians" could not...should not... ever admit to having. This place was my silo, my undisclosed location; my private asylum where I tucked away every truth I believed would be too much for the society of the "Blessed & Highly Favored (B&HF)" to handle. And because I wanted so desperately to be one of them (the B&HF), I believed I could not speak about my personal desolation. I could not verbalize my unchristian-like despondency. How could I? I was in church every time the doors were opened. I was there for every meeting, serving on every committee, and giving in the tithes and offering. Now how in the world could I say out loud that I was broken and breaking?

What kind of judgment would I have received in a transparent moment of revealing that I struggled to come to every church service and I dreaded serving on every committee and I always felt worse driving home than before I came. How could I say that? How could I keep my B&HF status if I acknowledged something was wrong? Church was supposed to fix me – wasn't it?

So, in an effort to keep my "platinum member" status, I painted on a smile. My Sunday-go-to-meeting suits presented the perfect disguise. My carefully constructed religious jargon concealed my truth. My artificial demeanor and persona camouflaged my reality. By all intents and purposes, I had become "The Great Pretender" and I was good at it - so I dare not blow my cover. How could I?

How could I tell them that I was really experiencing pain that made it difficult for me to inhale and exhale without feeling as though every breath was drawing life from me instead of my breaths giving life to me? Metaphorically speaking, although I inhaled, it seemed exhaling was excruciating, so I held everything inside.

The antagonistic pain made it difficult for me to sleep. So, most nights I merely tossed and turned in agony trying to buffer my thoughts with scattered prayers for peaceful rest. If I did manage to doze, when morning came and I awoke, I felt only intense sorrow that I had; and then, I began the process all over again. The pain made it difficult for me to eat, so I did not. In the process, I lost more than nourishment and weight. I lost balance, energy, and vitality. Most of all, I had come to the place where I lost my desire to be sustained – to continue – to go on.

So here I sat in the middle of my bedroom floor - a frail 107 pound skeletal shell of the person I used to be. Fleeting thoughts passed through my head without pausing long enough for my mind to grasp. I felt the illusion of a spinning room, leaving me dizzy while sitting completely still. My head ached. My stomach ached. My gums even ached – a symptom of mal-nourishment. I could literally feel life as it was leaking out through my pores and vaporizing into nothingness. But strangely enough, it did not matter. It did not matter because at this point in my life, all I could think about was …Death. In fact, fixation on my death was the thing that had brought me to my room at this point in time. I was here on a mission. Terminating this present life, this horrific state of being had crept its way to the top of my agenda and had become my solution for immediate relief. I was tired; so very, very tired. So, this was it. Today was the day. Grabbing a thought from here and there, I went through the plan in my head over and over again of how I was going to end my suffering.

My two small children were in their bedrooms on the other side of the house. They were occupied with games and television so they were content. With my limited capacity, I reasoned that now would be the perfect time because it was close to 4:30 p.m. and their father would be home by 5:00 p.m. so they would not have to be alone for

COUNTERFEIT

a very long time. I further reasoned that I did not want the dying process to be prolonged so I determined the quickest way to accomplish my goal. The only question that remained was whether or not I was going to leave a note explaining my decision.

If I left one, what would it say? How could I adequately explain what I was feeling and the reason I had come to this conclusion? Do I leave a note apologizing? If so, how could I explain this choice as one that was the best solution? What would the person finding the note think of me? I did not want to try to explain. So the note was out – there was no need.

My previous opposition to having a gun in the house had now turned into an opportunity. Although, I was not a skilled marksman, I believed I knew enough to accomplish the task, which had become what I reasoned to be my only option. So, I mustered up enough energy to push myself up off the floor to get to the closet where the gun was kept. It was securely locked in a box and was not loaded. As if to hide myself from myself, I closed the blinds and turned off the lights. I collected the box from the shelf and brought it back with me to my same spot beside the bed. I opened the box slowly and stared at this piece of metal that would undo everything. Before I ever touched it, I just stared.

Finally, I picked up the gun and opened the chamber and loaded it with the bullets that were also in the box. I am not sure why I believed I needed all of the bullets in the chamber. Perhaps they each represented a part of me, which I believed needed to die. After loading, I just held the gun in my hand. The tears began to pour like rain from black clouds that had been looming overhead as a warning that a storm was coming. The tears were not because I was having second thoughts about what I was going to do. I wept from the torment inside that had brought me to this point – to this place – to the conclusion of my life's story – to the end.

I had totally surrendered and given-in to the heaviness of my life. My entire body felt like an enormous weight that had become too unbearably difficult to carry around. My soul shook. And in my ears was the deafening rattle of the chains that held it in slavery. It had become too difficult to keep smiling when there was really nothing behind the smile. It had become too difficult to keep laughing when the humor in every aspect of my life had been lost. It was too difficult to continue to try to say the "right things" to the "right people" in and effort to continue to have them see you in the "right light." It had become just too difficult. It was too difficult to get out of bed every morning. It was too difficult to keep walking around with my inside twisted in knots from the deep, dark sadness I felt all the time. It was too difficult and no matter what I did, I could not make it go away. It was too difficult and I did not want to live another day.

I gathered myself and assumed the position. I sat up erect, with my left hand planted firmly on the floor, as if to anchor myself for what was to come. With my right hand, I raised the gun to my ear and letting the tip of the barrel rest there before tightening my grip on the handle and the trigger.

As I took in a deep breath – the one that I believed would be my last, I heard a loud rustling coming down the hall that led to my bedroom. Immediately, I dropped my hand, threw the gun in the box and quickly shoved it under the bed behind me. In a flash, my bedroom door flew open with swiftness and noise that seemed like it had been kicked off its hinges. However, kicking in a door was impossible because my son was too young and his frame was too tiny to break down a door. Yet, there he stood in front of me. His countenance was one I had never seen on his face before. In a peculiar way, it was filled with intention – a sense of purpose – a special mission and there was nothing child-like about it.

As I remained seated on the floor beside my bed, His eyes locked with mine. And with words that sprang forth like rivers of life, he yelled in the loudest voice he could muster, "Mommy! I may not be able to give you everything you need, but you will always have my love!" After a moment's pause and eyes still locked with mine, he turned and walked out of the room as swiftly as He came.

As time stood still…I saw my life flash before me. No, not the life that I had lived, but rather the life I still had left to live. And like fire in my blood, I sensed the burning conviction of my own selfishness. Like a hearse, my "me-ism" had brought me to this place and awaited my death so that it could carry me to a grave in which I had now spent years digging for myself. I broke… As though I was an attendee at my own funeral, I felt shrouded in the indescribable grief associated with the loss of a life unlived – a life with so much ahead – a life filled with purpose and destiny – a life filled with promise.

My son's words snapped me back into reality – a new reality. What I saw in his eyes transported me to a greater truth. Truth: the thing that had eluded me for far too long. Truth: the component of life that was really the sustainer of life. Truth: the element of my core that had been lost in years past. But now, here I sat, face-to-face with a very simple truth…the only truth that really mattered in the moment – I was loved – I was loved unconditionally. And in that instant, I knew it. I knew deep down in the crevices of every place I hurt. I knew it in each individual crack in my soul. I knew it in every fractured piece of my heart. I knew it in every wounded part of my spirit. I knew. Beyond my ability to fully understand, I had been given this incredible gift of knowing. I knew that I had encountered God. I knew that I had been given a new beginning.

However, emerging from the grip of death and seeking to set out on a different path, three questions hovered over my life. These were the three questions God asked the first human inhabitants on the earth. These were the questions that were asked in "the beginning" and these were the same questions being asked in my beginning - "Where Are You?" "Who Told You That You Were Naked?" "What Is This You Have Done?"

In attempting to answer these three questions, I was completely unaware that these questions would serve to introduce me to the "real" me. These would be the questions that would transport me back to my own genesis to meet *The Woman* that would bring me face-to-face with myself. These questions would be the questions that would expose the lies that covered the naked truth.

Thus, it is the intent of this book to encourage you to go deeply into the recesses of your own soul to answer these questions for yourself. I am here with you as you proceed. So let us walk this journey - together.

Before we attempt to answer a question, we should pause for a moment and consider why the question is being asked in the first place.

The Woman

The foundation of this book is built upon a glimpse into the life of "The Woman" we meet in Genesis. Many have called her "Eve". But for the sake of seeing ourselves in her life, she will remain nameless as we come to see her and know her simply as ourselves.

She is our beginning. She is the shadow of our existence. She is the side of us that has always been with us. Her image emerges with every glance we take in the mirror. She is the materialization of our creation and our purpose on the earth. Created from a rib, she is the bone found in our backs. She is the power of our weaknesses and she is the strength of our struggles. She is our voices, or the absence thereof. The Woman is us and we are the woman.

So...we dare not judge her. We dare not look upon her with contempt. Instead, we embrace her and we learn from her experience. We listen to her story and we seek to understand her journey.

We place ourselves in her position, in her conversations, and in her outcome. Why? Because she is us

and we are her and she holds the key to our authenticity -
The Woman.

Counterfeit - **coun·ter·feit**

adj. 1. Made in imitation of what is genuine with the intent to defraud

PART ONE:

Where Are You?

Before We Start...

A façade, a front, a masquerade, a fake – Are these the words that describe your life? Wait! Before you close this book and put it down, please stay with me for a moment. I know it may be difficult to admit because these are not the adjectives you would commonly use when asked for a description of your life. This is not the way you would normally introduce yourself. These are not words you would typically include on your resume or write in your autobiography. These are not even words that others would use to describe your life in light of what they have seen you accomplish, how they have watched you excel, or how much they know you really, really love God.

Instead, these words are the "ugly" words – the ones we choose to keep hidden and the ones we desperately guard, hoping they are never uncovered for fear of being exposed. These are the silent words. The ones left unspoken. Yet, they are there, embedded in the recesses of our minds. These are the words that rise to the surface of our thinking and settle in our gut each time we flash the huge "church smile" across our face in the middle of telling someone how "Blessed & Highly Favored!" we are – when all the while we hear in our spirit the quiet whispers of our own lies.

These hushed words show up in the mirror when we look at ourselves. We see with our eyes a self-manufactured picture of perfection – every hair in place, flawlessly beautiful makeup, and outfits that are super-model-ready. But, on the other hand, there is another face looking back at us, a body sporting an unseen garment of heaviness, the weight of which exists just below the surface of what is seen in our reflection. Yet, in the midst of the cover-up, the emotional turmoil, and the dualistic lifestyle, these words are the ones we dare not bring to the light because we would run the risk of letting others in on our well-kept secret – "I really am not who you think I am."

Consequently, we use our energy guarding the secret with our life, or rather in spite of our life. We become players of the game and masters of disguise – while drowning in the same water we have allowed others to believe we walk on. And somewhere along the way, we have convinced ourselves that the high price we pay for our external performance at the expense of our internal disintegration is worth it. So we continue our performances to audiences of many. We perform for those who love us. We perform for those who hate us. We perform for those who are completely indifferent concerning us. Encore, after encore, we return to the stage for these audiences, drooling over their applause, longing for their acceptance, or to capture their attention, while totally neglecting our sole obligation to only play to an audience of One.

We curtsy and bow in response to the temporary high of adulation. We look frantically for the "thumbs up" from our harshest critics. We linger on stage only to find that when the scene ends and the curtain closes and the crowd goes away, like a costume, we lay down the persona and come face-to-face with ourselves. Who is that person? Where does she belong? Where is her place in this world? Where does she fit? What is her purpose? What has she been sent to this world to accomplish? What is her value? What is her worth?

These are the questions that bombard our minds. But before we can stop long enough to give a response, we hear the crowd gathering again for another show. And, because we have grown accustomed to only brief intermissions of sincere contemplation of our life, we rise with vigor for the next act – Lights, Camera, Action – We're on! Separating ourselves from ourselves, we trade our wholeness for the allure of the crowd, never even recognizing the tragedy of our counterfeit response.

But here is the thing…The journey to authenticity and answering the questions life poses requires brutal honesty. It requires work. We cannot expect to get to an authentic response if we are unwilling to confront the fraudulent workings of our life. While many of us fear confrontation or try to avoid it at all costs, recapturing yourself is worth the encounter. It is worth confronting yourself. The *real* you has been covered long enough. The *real* you has lingered in the background while you have worn "the other you" like Cover Girl makeup – while knowing deep within that it is not all "Easy…Breezy…

Beautiful." The *real* you longs to break through. The real you longs to be free.

So now is your time. It is your time to move from a life of counterfeit living and to unleash your authenticity. It is your time to celebrate your uniqueness and to release yourself from the pressure to be like...to do it like...to act like...to appear like...or to pretend like...you are anything other than your truth. It is your time to uncover your naked truth. Now is your time! Now is your time...

CHAPTER ONE:
In the Beginning

A s a grandmother of two of the most amazing grandsons in the universe, one of my favorite things to do with them is to tell them completely off-the-cuff, made-up stories of dinosaurs, castles, horses, and brave kings that always save the day. All of these wonderfully creative stories begin with, "Once upon a time, in a far-away land..." The goal is to grab their attention and imagination and to transport them back into a place of long, long ago.

I know that you are not a one or three-year old and that you probably have no interest in entertaining stories from long, long ago. I am sure you are at the point in your life where you probably want to forget your past and leave it all behind. Well, I am not going to let you! While I am not an advocate of living in the past, I do believe that there are times when it is necessary to revisit the past so that we can extract the valuable lessons that are always present in our past experiences. Those times of trauma, hurt, shame, guilt, abuse, rejection, pain, and humiliation that are a tragic part of our yesterday have within them lessons and assignments that contain the power to rescue us when we face challenges in our today.

Digging through the rubble of our "once upon a time" often facilitates our understanding of where it all went wrong, but most importantly, where it all began. Therefore, as we embark upon our journey together through the pages of this book, I believe it is needful for us to go back to the beginning – all the way back to where it all started. Over the next few chapters, we will establish the context for our journey together through this book. So, let us begin together at the beginning...

Genesis

In the dictionary, Genesis is defined as, "The coming into being of something; the origin." In the book of Genesis, the first chapter opens with, "In the beginning..." From there, we become the captive audience of the God of the universe as he takes center stage in the midst of nonexistence and creates the world and mankind. Through the 31 verses of the first chapter of Genesis, we witness the launch of everything that was conceived in the mind of God even before its dramatic implementation as a world. These verses provide us the opportunity to take a step into the space of nothingness with God and journey through the portals of time to arrive at a destination completely surrounded by all he intended it to be.

Through the Scriptures, we watch as the Creator lights the hemisphere, fashions the terrain by separating water from the sky, and creates seas and dry land. We observe as he separates night from day and as he fills the seas and land with living creatures. And, after his marvelous creations, he admires it and calls it good. Everything he intentionally creates, he calls, good – He calls the beginning good.

"Good" Beginnings

In the beginning... What a powerful concept when we drop it into the context of our own lives. How often do we stop to consider our own..."In the beginning"? Do we allow our minds to take us beyond our moment of conception all the way back to the truth that even before the foundation of the world we were already conceived in the mind of God? Do we reflect on the truth that before our entry into world we already existed? Do we recognize that we were on the mind of God prior to the formation of any element of creation? Do we grasp the fact that our mother's womb was only a stopping point between God's intention concerning us and our arrival on the earth?

Ephesians 1:4 tells us that "Long before he laid down earth's foundations, he had us in mind, had settled on us as the focus of his love, to be made whole and holy by his love" (MSG). What a mind-boggling reality! There has never been a time – never a time in history when God was not thinking about us. And those thoughts were all good.

We see proof of this fact in the first chapter of Genesis. As God created all things that were created – day, night, sky, stars, land, plants, trees, and living creatures , he did so by merely speaking the words, "Let there be…" and immediately everything he spoke came into being.

However, before God created mankind, he took a very different approach than the one he had taken when he created other things. You see, in his sovereignty and power he could have simply remained consistent with his pattern of just speaking the words, "Let there be…" and mankind would have instantaneously appeared just as day, night, sky, stars, land, plants, trees, and living creatures had done over the course of six days. Instead, before the creation of mankind, God deliberated. He entered into consultation and collaboration with himself (the Trinity) as he stated, "Let us make mankind" (Genesis 1:26 - NIV). It is in this statement that we get the first glimpse of the heart of God concerning mankind.

It is here God pauses as he unveils his plan to create what has been conceived in his mind before the beginning of time. It is here that we see the intentionality of God. We see his desire to create something that would be unlike any other thing he had created prior to this time – Man.

However, God does not end his statement with "Let us make mankind." He continues his discourse by stating, "…in our image, in our likeness" (Genesis 1:26 - NIV). And from his likeness, God created male and female – man and woman (Genesis 1:27).

Imagine that! In the beginning, God created us with all of the attributes, characteristics, and qualities that existed in the Trinity. He created us in a true resemblance and representation of himself. We were created as a reflection of himself. We were created out of his essence - out of the very nature of who he is. We were created to be the quintessential complement of his existence. "Fearfully and wonderfully" he crafted us as a beautiful replica of his likeness - so our "In the beginning" has always been with him – it has always looked liked him. His thoughts about us have always been rooted in his love for us and his perfect desire and plan for us to be complete and set apart for him. And it was good. It was all good.

CHAPTER TWO:

Living the Good Life

I magine life in this garden. The man and the woman were surrounded by the stunning beauty of all God had created. It was the first "planned neighborhood" of sorts. They had amenities galore and a lifestyle of plenty. They were cared for, provided for, and sustained by everything that existed in their environment - they had everything they needed. And to top it all off, they could enjoy the vastness of the blessings of the garden completely naked.

Nakedness for the Man and the Woman was a blessed symbolism of their unembellished way of life. Their nakedness was never intended to be a burden – it was a gift from God – a status given to them freely for their delight and for their perfect alignment with all God had created. Their nakedness was included amongst the things God created in which he called "very good" (see Genesis 1:31). More importantly, because their nakedness was a gift from God, they were not embarrassed by their unclothed existence (see Genesis 2:25). They enjoyed the freedom of living exposed in front of God and all of his creation.

These human Beings made in the image of God existed in the liberty and openness of surroundings designed for their pleasure. Life in the Garden allowed them to live uncovered, open, and free…At least in the beginning…

With Freedom Comes Responsibility

Life in the garden for the Man and the Woman came with one stipulation. God gave them access to every part of the garden. From end-to-end, they could enjoy the plants, the animals, the streams, the flowers, and the trees, all except for one tree – The tree of the knowledge of good and evil (see Genesis 2:17). Yet, even though the Man and the Woman had access to all God had created, all he had done, and all he had intended - all it took was one conversation to completely undo his plans.

The Conversation, The Action, The Result (Genesis 3:1-13)

> [1] The serpent was the shrewdest of all the wild animals the LORD God had made. *One day he asked the woman, "Did God really say you must not eat the fruit from any of the trees in the garden?"*
> [2] "Of course we may eat fruit from the trees in the garden," the woman replied.
> [3] "It's only the fruit from the tree in the middle of the garden that we are not allowed to eat. God

said, 'You must not eat it or even touch it; if you do, you will die.'"

⁴ "You won't die!" the serpent replied to the woman.

⁵ "God knows that your eyes will be opened as soon as you eat it, and you will be like God, knowing both good and evil."

⁶ The woman was convinced. She saw that the tree was beautiful and its fruit looked delicious, and she wanted the wisdom it would give her. So she took some of the fruit and ate it. Then she gave some to her husband, who was with her, and he ate it, too.

⁷ At that moment their eyes were opened, and they suddenly felt shame at their nakedness. So they sewed fig leaves together to cover themselves.

⁸ When the cool evening breezes were blowing, the man and his wife heard the LORD God walking about in the garden. So they hid from the LORD God among the trees.

⁹ Then the LORD God called to the man, "Where are you?"

¹⁰ He replied, "I heard you walking in the garden, so I hid. I was afraid because I was naked."

¹¹ "Who told you that you were naked?" the LORD God asked. "Have you eaten from the tree whose fruit I commanded you not to eat?"

¹² The man replied, "It was the woman you gave me who gave me the fruit, and I ate it."

¹³ Then the LORD God asked the woman, "What have you done?" "The serpent deceived me," she replied. "That's why I ate it."

These turn of events found in Genesis set the stage for our journey together through the remaining pages of this book. I invite you to continue to walk with me as we delve more deeply into the conversation, the action, and the result. While this will not be an easy journey and one that may cause you great discomfort and fill you with an intense desire to close these pages, I ask that you remain. I ask that you allow the inner you to speak to your mind, your will, and your emotions. I ask that you listen to your soul's cry for freedom. I ask that you see this journey as a commitment to pursue life, so that you can step away from the grip of death. I ask that you proceed with the intention to uncover the lies that have covered your truth. Come with me...

CHAPTER THREE:
Never Talk To Strangers

In Genesis 1:13, the woman's statement is intriguing, "The serpent deceived me, and I ate." The Woman blames the serpent for lying to her. She takes no responsibility for 1) *having a conversation* with the serpent and 2) *believing* the lie. The Woman believed the lie even though she already knew what God had instructed - she knew the truth. Therefore, trading the truth for a lie, she became the victim of the biggest con of the enemy. The enemy painted a beautiful picture of what choosing another way would look like. He tampered with the woman's imagination and manipulated the vision of what she saw to reflect something he suggested would be better. But the reality is that it was all just an illusion of grandeur.

However, before we bash the Woman, there are times when we ourselves know what is true…we know what is right. Yet, we are enticed and drawn away to embrace the complete opposite of that truth. We entertain conversations with others and ourselves that cause us to deviate from that deep place of knowing that resides on the inside of us. We walk away from the certainty of what we know and what we believe to follow a deceptive path in which we have been convinced will lead us to our "happily ever after." And, how does this happen? Let's examine the process.

In Genesis 3:1, the serpent begins his conversation with the woman by asking her one question, "Did God really say you must not eat the fruit from any of the trees in the garden?" Notice the first four words of the question, "Did God really say…?" In a very cunning and crafty manner, the serpent interjected an instance for the Woman to question the truth. However, the Woman responded to the serpent by stating what she knew and what she believed in that moment – "Of course we may eat fruit from the trees in the garden," the Woman replied. "It's only the fruit from the tree in the middle of the garden that we are not allowed to eat. God said, 'You must not eat it or even touch it; if you do, you will die'" (Genesis 3:2-3).

With certainty and great confidence the Woman responded to the question. She spoke with great authority and complete assurance that what she was stating was the truth. The Woman knew the truth – she could even repeat the truth. There was no doubt in her mind. Why should there be? God had never lied to them.

Nevertheless, with all she knew, she still engaged in the conversation and she listened to serpent as he stated, "You won't die! God knows that your eyes will be opened as soon as you eat it, and you will be like God, knowing both good and evil" (Genesis 3:4-5). *And the woman was convinced* (Genesis 3:6).

The woman moved from what she knew, to being *convinced* that the *truth* was somehow less than what she should be content with. In that moment, the truth was somehow not good enough. There was more. She became convinced that she was missing out on something. This one conversation with a stranger had persuaded her to step away from everything she knew and believed, from everything that had been a part of her designed way of life, from everything that was created for her, and from everything that God called good.

It was here where her participation in what seemed to be a harmless conversation, completely shifted the course of her life. This conversation totally changed her destiny. And, the tragedy is that the Woman was completely unaware of the deadly influence emerging from her dialogue with this stranger. She did not know that this "innocent" talk had camouflaged within each word, the trappings of death - no, not physical death – but the power to kill her truth, her spirit, and her authenticity. She did not know that with every word exchanged with this stranger, she was losing a piece of herself. She was losing the very essence of who she was created to be. Like a slow leak in a tire, her words with the stranger were setting her up for a complete depletion of what had been placed on the inside of her. But, the truth of the matter is, this conversation was her choice.

The conversations we have entertained over the course of our lives have been our choice. We have chosen to give-in to the seducing voices spewing from people, places, and things around us. In spite of the truth we knew, we talked, and we listened.

But, They Didn't Look Strange To Me...

Herein lies the danger of entertaining conversations with "strangers" – or rather people that show up in our lives that are foreign to our lives. In other words, those who we really have not taken the time to get to know beyond their physical appearance, color, age, marital status, socioeconomic status, education, vocation, religious affiliation, family make-up, and many other demographics.

These strangers are those with whom we have never communicated beyond the superficial. We have not discerned their heart, their intent, or their motives. We have not asked God about their presence in our lives. We have not consulted him about the purpose they are there to serve. We have simply assumed that it is safe and we open ourselves to them – never really knowing them at all. We open ourselves to their influence, their motives, their agendas, and their plans. And once open, we leave space and our vulnerability for whatever the stranger has to offer.

I know you may be saying, "But they didn't look strange to me." Well, let me take a moment to provide a profile of a stranger. A stranger is one who is:

- Often unassuming - not flashing "red flags" at first site
- Very engaging - showing interest in what it is you have to say, what it is you do, and what it is you like - It's all about you
- Extremely complimentary - filling your ears with the amazing things you want to hear about yourself and how wonderful you are

- Overwhelmingly smooth - causing you to desire some or many of the qualities they display
- Charismatically charming - exuding energy that draws you in and captivates your attention

While none of these descriptions are negative in and of themselves, when they are the characteristics of someone who is a stranger, or rather outside of the purpose and path for your life, someone with impure intentions, and someone with a focus on deceiving, these same characteristics are deadly. Yet, these are the same characteristics that entice us into counterfeit living.

Forbidden Fruit

Our entry into counterfeit living begins with knowing the truth, yet stepping away from what we know because we have been convinced by the lie of "more". Tantalized by all that the world dangles in front of us, we listen to its alluring enticements for bigger, better, and more. We are led to believe that we should and can have it all. In our hunger for something God never intended for us to eat, we follow the trail of forbidden fruit, believing that this path will lead us to something more glorious than what we already have. We are ensnared by a desire to "gain the world" – and it is in that moment, we allow the lie and lust for more to lead us away, far, far away from the truth.

But nothing good comes from this lie...absolutely nothing. This lie strips our souls of the security and confidence found in the truth. This lie seduces us and robs us of the innocence that truth gives. This lie violates the boundaries of protection that have been established by the truth. This lie changes the very nature of who we are, while morphing us into something we never imagined we would become. And this lie infringes upon our nakedness before God and causes us to create coverings...the ones we learn to live our lives hiding behind. But most tragically, the longer we remain in this state of being, the lies we live become our reality and we ultimately become unaware of the fact that the truth no longer remains.

The Truth Has Left the Building

When we let go of the truth in our lives, we make space for all that is counterfeit to take its place. Trading in the *certainty* and *comfort* found in truth, we opt for the uncertainty and discomfort of the unknown. Oddly enough, we convince ourselves that this is the walk of faith. But, here is a NEWS FLASH, faith cannot exist outside of truth. I define truth as *the tangible knowing and belief about who God is and everything he has spoken and created*. Therefore, when we release this knowing and belief for substitute knowledge, truth cannot remain.

Nevertheless, when truth leaves, we become vulnerable. We become susceptible. We become gullible. We become an easy target and an alluring prey. When we depart from the truth, we sacrifice everything God called "good" and we invite in the toxic workings of deception. But most importantly, when the truth leaves us, authentic living leaves us and we become walking shells, void of all

God intended for us have and for us to be. Then, no longer covered by the truth, we spiral, because nothing remains to hold us in place. In the process, we lose ourselves and take on identities that were never intended for us to have.

CHAPTER FOUR:

A Place Called "Here"

Brought into this world and sustained in their nakedness, it was not until the Man and the Woman deviated from their perfect alignment with God's will that they became aware of their nakedness and felt ashamed of what they saw. To them, they were no longer merely naked bodies, but their nakedness now symbolized something they believed needed to be hidden. In an instant of yielding to temptation, they experienced immediate grief associated with the loss of all that was theirs. And now their nakedness became a mark of guilt and distress. In an effort to try to hide their overwhelming conviction, they did what any rational transgressor would do – they hid. The Man and the Woman sewed together leaves to cover themselves.

Covered with leaves, they heard God walking in the garden. I can only imagine the panic they felt when they heard his footsteps, saw the light of his presence, and felt the power of his omnipotence.

I can only imagine their desperation as they tried to camouflage their state of being by using leaves to blend in with their surroundings in an effort to get away. I can picture the frantic search for leaves, and more leaves, and more and more leaves. With rapid heartbeats and distressed scurries, they planned their strategy to cover it all up. But then, God shows up. And not only does he show up, he asks a question.

He asks the question that would stop them in their tracks, the question that caused an immediate lump to form in their throats, and the one that tied their stomachs in knots. God simply asked, **"Where are you?"** The man's response..."I heard your voice in the garden, and I was afraid because I was naked; and I hid myself" (Genesis 3:10). However, there was simply silence from the Woman.

Does any of this sound familiar? Think about your response to God when we get any inkling that God is looking for us. You may ask, "How do I know when God is looking for me?" We know when we get that feeling in our gut that things are just not right. We know when the restlessness in our spirit grows so intense that we find it difficult to remain comfortable. We know when everything in us - our mind, will, and emotions puts us on high alert that we are grossly misaligned with God's plan for our creation. We know when things around us seem to start falling apart. We know when we seem to find no peace. We know when we begin to feel heavy, overloaded, and COVERED. And if we will admit it, our response to all of this is usually - silence.

Shhh....

When we remain silent, while knowing the truth, our silence keeps us hidden. It is our unwillingness to speak or to acknowledge what we know that keeps the real us barricaded inside ourselves. It is the stifled voice of truth that causes us to linger in a state of secrecy, while completely disregarding the fact that silence kills.

When we are silent about the truth, we make room for other things inside of us to die. Our courage dies, our confidence dies, and our genuineness dies, as we give space for other things to live - despair, hopelessness, and helplessness. Remaining silent robs us of joy and freedom. It steals our ability to use our voices to speak into existence those things that our heart desires. Being silent sabotages the "good success" we were intended to have.

Silence causes us to question while finding no answers. Silence weakens us and sucks the life out of us. Being silent paralyzes us and keeps us mired deeply in our dysfunction. Silence gives others permission to control us, manipulate us, use us, and abuse us, while blinding us to the fact that as we are silent, we leave others around us vulnerable to its toxic manifestations. This silence is not golden. There is nothing about it that resembles beauty. In the end, it only serves to leave us void of power and it keeps us fearful, covered, and in hiding.

I heard you. I was afraid. I was naked. I hid myself.

"Where are you?" was the first biblically documented question God ever asked. Why? What was the significance of this question? Why would an all-knowing, all-powerful, and ever-present God find the need to ask such a question in the first place? Of course God knew where the man was and he knew exactly what the man was doing at the very moment he asked the question. Yet, he stilled asked. He stilled asked despite the fact that he had created the man and knew everything about him. He still asked even though he had created the garden and he knew every nook and cranny it contained. He still asked, already knowing the answer to his question.

So, why ask? I believe he asked the question not for his own knowledge, but rather for the man's. He asked so that he could give the man an opportunity to pose the same question to himself, "Where am I?" He asked so that he could give the man a moment to consider just how far away he had moved from God's plan for his life.

Can you relate to that place? It is the place where you feel so very far away from the path you know you were created to travel? It is the place where you wake up one day and the question racing through your head is, "How did I get here?" It is the place where you feel separated from the "right thing" while the "wrong thing" pulls you farther and farther away. It is the place of spiraling hopelessly out of control while desperately wanting to stop the fall yet feeling nothing is there to catch you.

It is that place where you cannot believe you are there. It is the place where you told yourself time and time again you would never go. It is that place where you have stood in judgment of others that have gone there before you. Now here you are – in that very place. And the haunting question that lingers in the back of your mind is, "Where am I?" Understand this, by the time you come to the place of asking yourself the question, "Where am I?" - You are also acknowledging that you are in a location you were never meant to be.

The Man responded to God's question of "Where are you?" by saying, "I heard you in the garden, and I was afraid because I was naked; so I hid" Genesis 3:10 (NIV). Adam offers God what he believes to be three perfectly good reasons for hiding: 1.) hearing God approaching, 2.) being afraid, and 3.) being naked. However, what is most interesting is that Adam never stated *where he was*, he only stated *what he was doing.* Do any of the Man's reasons for hiding sound familiar to you? Reflect for a moment over the course of your own life. What has been your response when you recognized that you are grossly misaligned with the will, plan, and purpose of God? Did you try to escape God's presence? Or let me put it this way, did you stop praying? Did you stop reading your bible and setting aside quiet time? Did you stop attending church on a regular basis? Did you make it a point to stay away from certain Christians because you felt quite sure that they could "see you" or see your state of being? Has the question, "Where are you?" ever tapped you on the shoulder, or awakened you in the middle of the night, or produced knots in the middle of your gut each time you heard it? Can you relate to Adam and the reasons he gave God? Think about it for a moment.

How Did I Get Here?

Consider this. At no point in the discourse with God did the Man say, "Here I am." He only offered God insight into what he was doing. You may be asking, what's the difference? I am glad you asked. "Where are you?"- requires that we provide specifics about our location. The question calls to the places that are deep on the inside of us that we have kept in hiding. It calls for deep introspection. It calls for us to assess everything in us and around us. It beckons us to come forward and come straight with our true position - our true status. Thus, in answering the question, we must begin with, "I am here."

When we begin with what we are *doing*, it allows us to remain in hiding because we can stand behind our activity and our business. However, "I am here" requires honesty, transparency, and complete exposure. In other words, this is our opportunity to say to God I have nothing to hide. I want you to see everything. I want you to know everything. Nothing is hidden in this moment. I give you my naked truth. I have nothing to hide. I have nowhere to run. I am here, God, and I want you to see me.

The place to begin this process is by addressing the question, "How did I get here?" This question serves as our personal locator. Others can ask us many questions to which we have very little difficulty responding:

How are you doing? Fine!

How was your weekend? Great!

How is the weather? Awesome!

How is your family? Wonderful!

Yet, when we consider the question asked by God, "Where are you?" Gulp...uh, uh, uh, uh...

So what do you do with the question? How do you respond? Far too often we ask ourselves the question, "How did I get here?" While this is a wonderful question, it does not address where "here" is. Unless we can identify where we are, we will never be able to truly answer how we got there. It would be like expecting our GPS system to give us directions to our desired destination without ever turning on the power and allowing the system to access our current location. If we do not know where we are, it is going to be a very long and slow process for us to get to where we are supposed to be. Therefore we must be brutally honest about our "here" - What does it look like? What does it feel like? What does it smell like? What does to sound like?

There have been occasions over the course of my life where I wondered how I could spiral so out of control, stoop to an unintended level, cross my own boundaries, or transgress my own limitations. In each instance, the first question that ran rampantly through my mind was always, "How did I get here?" I never imagined that my life would go this way. What happened? What went wrong? For many of us, "here" is the destination that the enemy has orchestrated for our destruction. It is the place that is the epitome of our loss of power, our loss of identity, and our loss of self. "Here" is the place where we are so deeply mired in our mess that we dismiss ourselves from our dignity, our values, and our morals. "Here" is the place described in Luke 15:11-17:

¹¹ Jesus told them this story: "A man had two sons. ¹² The younger son told his father, 'I want my share of your estate now before you die.' So his father agreed to divide his wealth between his sons. ¹³ "A few days later this younger son packed all his belongings and moved to a distant land, and there he wasted all his money in wild living. ¹⁴ About the time his money ran out, a great famine swept over the land, and he began to starve. ¹⁵ He persuaded a local farmer to hire him, and the man sent him into his fields to feed the pigs. ¹⁶ The young man became so hungry that even the pods he was feeding the pigs looked good to him. But no one gave him anything.¹⁷ "When he finally came to his senses, he said to himself, 'At home even the hired servants have food enough to spare, and **here** I am dying of hunger!

"Here" is also a placed described in John 4:6-15:

⁶ Jacob's well was there; and Jesus, tired from the long walk, sat wearily beside the well about noontime. ⁷ Soon a Samaritan woman came to draw water, and Jesus said to her, "Please give me a drink." ⁸ He was alone at the time because his disciples had gone into the village to buy some food. ⁹ The woman was surprised, for Jews refuse to have anything to do with Samaritans. She said to Jesus, "You are a Jew, and I am a Samaritan woman. Why are you asking me for

adrink?"[10] Jesus replied, "If you only knew the gift God has for you and who you are speaking to, you would ask me, and I would give you living water." [11] "But sir, you don't have a rope or a bucket," she said, "and this well is very deep. Where would you get this living water? [12] And besides, do you think you're greater than our ancestor Jacob, who gave us this well? How can you offer better water than he and his sons and his animals enjoyed?" [13] Jesus replied, "Anyone who drinks this water will soon become thirsty again. [14] But those who drink the water I give will never be thirsty again. It becomes a fresh, bubbling spring within them, giving them eternal life." [15] "Please, sir," the woman said, "give me this water! Then I'll never be thirsty again, and I won't have to come **here** to get water." [16] "Go and get your husband," Jesus told her. [17] "I don't have a husband," the woman replied. Jesus said, "You're right! You don't have a husband— [18] for you have had five husbands, and you aren't even married to the man you're living with now. You certainly spoke the truth!"

In both of these instances, the place called "here" represents a place of dishonor and shame. It represents a level of degradation and humiliation. It represents a very dark place. It represents a place where we question, where we ponder, and where we wonder - How did I get here?

Like The Woman...

I n my own life, the darkness came in because I let it in. I gave the darkness my permission to occupy my space. And, with my permission, it came in through every spiritual portal I opened and allowed to remain open, accommodating its entrance:

My Ears

The very first verse of Chapter 3 of Genesis says, *The serpent was the shrewdest of all the wild animals the Lord God had made. One day he asked the woman, "Did God really say you must not eat the fruit from any of the trees in the garden?"* (NLT). What this Scripture does not say is, "…And the woman listened."

But, she did. She listened. She opened her ears to the serpent's voice. She opened her ears to a voice that was different from that of her Creator – a voice of a stranger. She attuned her ears to the selfishly calculating voice of the one whose only purpose was to summon her away from the plan and purpose of God. She listened to the voice that raised a question and introduced doubt in her mind. She listened. I listened.

I listened to that same voice. You may be familiar with it also. You know the one – the voice that whispers in your ear with high hopes that it will grab your attention and lure you in with its seductiveness. It is the voice that begins the conversation with you by asking, "Did God really say that?" It is the voice that calls you to compromise – calls you to rethink and second-guess the very things you believed you believed. It is the voice that offers you the option to justify and to excuse. It is the voice that invites you to release yourself from the stress and burden of accountability.

This voice is the one that entices you into reckless abandonment of your original design. This voice is the one that speaks the language of your unspoken and often forbidden desires. It is the voice that peaks your curiosity, tickles your flesh, and woos you beyond temptation into action. This voice is a subtle one – one that conceals its identity as it speaks through other *people*, through other *places*, and through other *things*:

Through People (Influence)

Influence is defined as, *A power affecting a person, thing, or course of events.* When we fall prey to the seductive workings operating through others in our lives, it is often in the form of negative influence. When we allow it, this misaligned influence is a powerful force which alters the course of our lives. As a result, our focus shifts from pleasing God to pleasing others and/or doubting God and believing others.

As we attune our ears to the voices of influence which we have allowed to form the circle around us, like a child seduced by the Pide Piper of Hamelin's mystical songs from his magic pipe, we follow. We follow not knowing where we are being led and too intoxicated to notice. Listening, we follow. We follow, leaving the original plan and the very blueprint for our existence. With each step, we are walking away from our destiny. With each step we are leaving behind our purpose, our passion, and our power as we morph into an unrecognizable version of ourselves – standing helplessly at the mercy of influence of others while responding on command to the "Power of They": What "they" think. What "they" say. How "they" feel. What "they" do. What "they" believe.

However, this insistent need to please slowly becomes a deadly disease to please. And although negative influences from others do not always appear to be negative, this type of influence is indeed a subtle destroyer. As we listen to the influential thoughts, opinions, and promptings from others and we receive them and incorporate them into our lives, we are inadvertently saying to God, "I'd rather please them than you, so I'm going to go with what's popular instead of what's planned."

The most lethal aspect of negative influence is that it often happens without our knowledge. While we are aware of the voices around us, we are not aware of their influence on us. Consider these indicators of negative influence:

1. When we are unable to muster up the courage to say "no" to a person when everything in us is screaming, yet we silence the noise of our opposition with our usual "yes" – we must check the influence.

2. When we trade the truth in exchange for telling lies because it is what another person wants to hear and we do not want to risk of displeasing them and losing the relationship, we must check the influence.

3. When we respond swiftly to the beck and call of someone else while neglecting our relationship with God and our own sense of well being, we must check the influence.

4. When our own needs become secondary because we have allowed others to convince us that their needs are more important, we must check the influence.

5. When we diminish our God-given gifts, talents and abilities because we have allowed others to convince us that using them, advancing, and accomplishing, is a waste of time because where we are is "just fine", we must check the influence.

6. When we give our all time and time again only to receive nothing in return, we must check the influence.

7. When we walk away from our own potential to grow and reach our goals and to walk in the purpose of God simply because we have surrounded ourselves with people who have no

desire to pursue their own, we must check the influence.

Allowing ourselves to be negatively influenced in anyway that is contrary to the God-power we have been given to lead our lives causes us to enter into a place of deep oppression. We become barricaded in and we are kept from the freedom that is ours. Consequently, we learn to listen to the rhythm of someone else's drum and we abandon our own as we move to the influence of the beat of another. And the beat goes on...

And so it was with me. Like an addiction, this "people pleasing" vice had me in its grip. Void of an authentic personal identity, I was a pathetic semblance of what I believed would be most acceptable to others (Others being the people who loved me and the people who did not love me, like me, or even come close). Yet, here I was – strung out – habitually; compulsively involved in a behavior that was keeping me from a life of sobriety.

While often overdosing on the façade of public approval, I was still strategizing a plan for how to get my next high. Binging, spiraling, railing out of control in the death-grip of a disease to please – one that was killing me softly, I yielded. Ignorant of my desperate need for intervention, I sought none. As a result, I remained in this toxic state of existence oppressed by a power that constantly lurked in the recesses of my mind.

Through Places (Fear)

It is the voice that binds us to places (churches, jobs, states, cities, communities, houses, etc.) long past our seasons while whispering reasons why we should stay, as our fruit withers on the vine right before our very eyes. And yet, we remain.

Why do we remain? Fear. When we give in to the seductive allure of power and position, we allow ourselves to become vulnerable to the fear of losing or missing out on something. In Genesis 3, when the serpent asked the woman, "Did God really say that you must not eat the fruit from any of the trees in the Garden?" (v-1) – he was setting her up to question whether or not she had all the power she really could have. While her response was, "Of course we may eat fruit from the trees in the garden, it's only the fruit from the tree in the middle of the garden that we are not allowed to eat. God said, 'You must not eat it or even touch it; if you do, you will die'" (v-3) – doubt was already entering in her mind. However, fear entered in when the serpent continued, "You won't die! God knows that your eyes will be opened as soon as you eat it, and you will be like God, knowing both good and evil" (v-5).

Where did fear come in? It entered in when she doubted and opened herself to be convinced that she was missing out on some form of power and position she could have had or should have had in the garden. Fear enthralled her mind, will, and emotions and caused her to believe that God was holding out on her and that she was going to miss out on something better if she did what He had commanded. In essence, she was tricked into staking her claim on a life better than the one ordained by God.

This is the same temptation we face. Although God gives us access to all He has purposed for our lives, we give in to the enemy's whispers which causes us to want more –

more of what He never intended for us to have – more of what He commanded us to stay away from – more of what can ultimately be the cause of our death. Yet, we still want more. Why? Because we have allowed ourselves to be convinced that power and position somehow increases our importance in the world. Therefore, we seek after it, we thirst for it and we will try to attain it by any means necessary, even if it means we give up everything God has promised to wholeheartedly pursue the one thing that was never a part of His plan for our lives.

Truthfully, the reason the enemy uses power and position as a bait to ensnare us is because it is a perfect decoy to cause us to move out of the will of God. In actuality, the strategy to move us out of God's will is not even about us as much as it is about the enemy's attempt to prove to God that He can cause us to move out of His will – with just one whisper – with just one question. When we willingly listen, we become a participant in the enemy's strategy.

Through Things (Manipulation)

It is the voice that causes us to become distracted, not just by the things that shine, sparkle, and glitter. But, we become distracted by other things, such as illicit relationships, toxic friendships, unhealthy drives to accomplish, a need to succeed (by any means necessary), and a daily deadly indulgence of me, myself, and I. This voice, the one that causes us to acquiesce, is the same voice that begins the process of the darkening of our lives.

When we are consumed with and by things, we are driven beyond making good decisions for our life. Rather than considering what would be good for us, we make choices based upon what we can get out of it – or in other words, what is good to us. We will even pass up the good and opt for the bad, simply because it seemingly has more to offer us. This way of operating draws us into a life of manipulation – searching for ways to use everything and everyone for our advantage, all in the pursuit of more, more, more, more. The consequence is that we lose our filters. We empty ourselves of our true selves and fill our capacity for rational and reasonable thinking with the indulgencies of this world. Always on the chase to fulfill the insatiable appetite for things, we become prowlers of sorts – strategically waiting for our next opportunity to capture the coveted prize – another thing.

It is the same enticements the Woman faced – the "You Can Have More" syndrome. But what about the cost? When we are striving for things, we are not considering the fact that we are also giving up some valuable part of ourselves to pursue what we think is better. Like the Woman, God has granted us access to blessings upon blessings and promises upon promises. However, the enemy of our souls causes us to only focus on the things we cannot and should not have. Is it because God is fixated on withholding "good things" from us? No, it is because he knows what is good for us. He is not trying to keep us from the good, he is trying to lead us toward the good. However, it us – we get in our own way and block our own success, while wondering why "things" just never seem to work out.

WHERE ARE YOU?

Your authentic response to this question is the first step in the process of stepping out of the darkness into the light of your truth. So, where are you at this very moment in your life? Be honest with yourself. Have you sensed God's presence around you? Have you felt that he was looking for you? Have you been coming up with ways to stay away from him because of the hidden areas in your life? Be very honest. This is your opportunity to acknowledge to yourself where you really are. What are the secret areas you have kept hidden from view? What are the areas that are misaligned with God's purpose and plan for your life? What are the "fearfully and wonderfully made" (Psalm 139:14) components of yourself that you have never allowed to be expressed? What are the lies that reside on the inside that you have never exposed to the light of truth? What are the areas of darkness where you dare not go, nor do you allow anyone else to enter? Take some dedicated and committed time to answer these questions. Listen for the answers and write down what you hear. How will you respond?

Reflection

_____

_____

_____

_____

_____

_____

_____

_____

_____

_____

_____

_____

_____

_____

_____

PART TWO:

Who Told You That
You Were Naked?

Before We Start...

Trying to hide my inadequacies was a way of life I acquired over time. However, because I was keenly aware that there were things that were "not quite right" in my spirit, I truly desired to be spiritual. Therefore, I ran to the one thing I believed would make it better and cure me of all my ills – Religion.

I lived a great portion of my life assuming that the two, religious and spiritual, were one in the same. But, my assumption was very wrong. In fact, after experiencing the negative trappings of religious thinking and behaving, I came to understand that there was a difference – an extreme difference between the two. "Religious" referring to a *belief* in God and "Spiritual" referring to *relating* to God.

I have **believed** in God for as long as I can remember. In fact, I can't recall a time when I didn't believe in God. However, my life in **relating** to God has evolved. It has grown over the years, over the months, over the weeks, over the days...while leaving room for moment-by-moment interaction with Him.

Relating to Him is the essence of my connection to the Source of my life. Relating to Him brings me into sweet communion with the One who desires my presence more than anyone else. Relating to Him causes me to want more, see more, do more and be…MORE. Relating to Him silences the noise of the external, while showing me just how little it matters in comparison to His plan and His purpose for me. His plan, the one that I will only realize as I relate to Him. His purpose, the one that while relating to Him, unfolds right before my very eyes.

In the midst of storms, trials, situations, circumstances, issues…whatever we call the adverse happenings of life, relating to Him positions me to ask, "God. Where are you?" Relating to Him allows me to hear Him when He answers…."I AM… right here.

However, recognizing our inadequacies is the greatest gift we can offer ourselves. Why is it important to admit our inadequacies? It is important because acknowledging that we have inadequacies draws us to a deeper understanding of our need for the amazing Grace of God in our lives. When we are honest about our shortcomings, we position ourselves for God's help. When we are honest, we take the pressure off ourselves to try to convince others that we are someone other than ourselves. When we are honest, we tackle the lie that the enemy has convinced us to believe over the course of our lives that who God created us to be is just not good enough – we need to be more than that.

In fact, lying to us has been the enemy's strategy since his conversation with the Woman. Convincing us to believe the lies fulfills his goal to hold us captive in pride, arrogance and pretense in a life of superficiality and disingenuous living. It is when we are not honest with ourselves, that we rob ourselves of the freedom of living our truth.

CHAPTER FIVE:

The Blame Game

The question of "Where are you?" leads us to the second question God asks. Let us revisit the conversation in Genesis 3:6-10:

> 6 The woman was convinced. She saw that the tree was beautiful and its fruit looked delicious, and she wanted the wisdom it would give her. So she took some of the fruit and ate it. Then she gave some to her husband, who was with her, and he ate it, too. 7 At that moment their eyes were opened, and they suddenly felt shame at their nakedness. So they sewed fig leaves together to cover themselves. 8 When the cool evening breezes were blowing, the man and his wife heard the LORD God walking about in the garden. So they hid from the LORD God among the trees. 9 Then the LORD God called to the man, "Where are you?" 10 He replied, "I heard you walking in the garden, so I hid. I was afraid

because I was naked." [11] **"Who told you that you were naked?"** the LORD God asked. "Have you eaten from the tree whose fruit I commanded you not to eat?" [12] The man replied, "It was the woman you gave me who gave me the fruit, and I ate it."

It is here where God asks the Man another very powerful question – "Who told you that you were naked?" (See Genesis 3:11, NIV). In other words, I believe God was asking the man, who told you that the state you were in was not good enough? Who told you that you needed to cover the very essence of who I created you to be? Who told you that you should be ashamed of who you are? Who told you that my plan for the way I purposed you to live your life was not sufficient?

And, what was the Man's response? Blame! He blamed God and he blamed the Woman. "The woman *you* put here with me – *she* gave me some fruit from the tree, and I ate it" (Genesis 3:12, NIV). In other words, he was saying, "God, you gave me this woman. I was doing just fine all by myself. But, no! That wasn't good enough for you. You had to go and create her and put her here with me. Now look at what she's made me do! The way I see it, the two of you need to own up to this whole mess because I had absolutely nothing to do with it! I thought she was just sharing her fruit with me and I was trying not to be rude. So I politely accepted. I had nothing to do with what happened next!" However, the man never answered the question. He never addressed what God was really asking him. Instead, he did what come easiest for him. He blamed.

It's Really Not My Fault

I know it sounds foolish when we hear the Man accusing God and the Woman. It sounds foolish when we hear the Woman concocting the original "The Devil made me do it" excuse. But, is it not foolish when we do these same things ourselves? How often do we cast blame for our actions and make attempts to take away the attention from ourselves. We identify the culprit, point the finger, and immediately assign ourselves the status of "victim". We let ourselves off the hook and try to convince God to do the same by offering him excuses and justification. But, as the blame is flowing from our lips, we fail to realize that we are writing our own permission slip to be excused from accountability. We become judge and jury of our actions with every intention to render ourselves a verdict of "not guilty."

With our authorized consent, we continue down a path of "allows". We *allow* the influence and opinions of people to cover us. We *allow* the allure of places to cover us. We *allow* the enticement of things to cover us. We *allow* tragedies and pain from our childhood to cover us. We *allow* hurts and disappointment from failed relationships to cover us. We allow how we have been mistreated to cover us. We *allow* the fear of "What if…?" to cover us. We *allow* rejection and despondency to cover us. We *allow* mistakes and regrets from our past to cover us. We *allow* bitterness and resentment to cover us. We *allow* the quest and striving for success to cover us. We *allow* judgmental attitudes and critical spirits to cover us. We *allow* pride to cover us. Yes, we allow all these things and so much more to provide a means by which we cover the very nakedness that was intended to be our gift from God. But what keeps us from owning our part in it? Why do we blame everyone and everything around us?

Blaming others for where we are and for what we have done is a covert form of hiding. The blame allows us to hide behind the excuse that it was someone else's fault. It allows us to create an illusion of our own innocence. Blaming others turns our focus to external activities so that we do not have to acknowledge our internal stuff.

However, the most detrimental aspect of blaming others is that it covers us. It causes us to "sew together fig leaves" (Genesis 3:7) to cover our guilt. It covers our authenticity. It covers our transparency. It covers the very nakedness that was our original gift from God. As a result, we become cloaked in leafy garments that only serve to cover the "real" us.

Come Out, Come Out, Wherever You Are

We were not created to wear leaves! Over time we have gathered leaves when we have been deceived. We have gathered leaves when we have believed lies and walked away from our authentic truth. Over time, we have gotten comfortable wearing those leaves – not even recognizing the degree to which our leaves are keeping us hidden from our truth – the truth of why we were created - The TRUTH that we were not created to go through life:

- covered in the leaves that have now become excuses for why we do the things we do;
- covered in the leaves that give us permission to remain where we are while finding comfort in the fact that as we look around, everyone else is covered;
- covered in the leaves that drain our passion, distort our purpose, and disconnect us from our power.

Because it was never God's plan for us to live covered, because he never purposed for us to live camouflaged, and because he never wrote it in our script for us to live in hiding, he comes looking for us. And he comes with questions.

He does not ask the questions because he does not know the answer. He asks the questions as an invitation for us to conduct our own self-assessment. He asks the questions so that we can begin to ask our own questions. He asks so that we can begin to find our own answers.

The truth of the matter is our coverings do not hide us from God. He sees and knows all. But, our coverings hide us from ourselves – rendering us unrecognizable. Even when looking at our own image in the mirror we see what we have made acceptable. We see the airbrushed version we have created for ourselves. We see our flaws removed, our imperfections altered, and our authenticity erased. We see a painted on smile – one that only represents the public persona we have dressed ourselves for. We see eyes that only look outward and never call us to look inward. We see ears that dismiss whisperings from a still, quiet voice of the Holy Spirit that wants desperately to grab our attention. We see mere casings of ourselves; while convincing ourselves that "looking good" is good enough. However, living covered sabotages the truth about our lives. As a result, we learn to live a distortion of the truth – completely relinquishing our power and influence, all because we have ignored, forgotten, been deceived, or never known the real truth of who we are.

Killing Me Softly

Over time, living a life of being covered begins to kill us; perhaps not physically, but certainly emotionally and spiritually. Living covered begins to suffocate us and takes from us of our ability to breathe, our ability to sense and feel life, and our ability to know happiness and joy. However, the most dangerous aspect of living covered is that the longer we live in this state of being, our ability to recognize our own dying process diminishes. We do not recognize that the things on the inside of us deposited there by God are slowly dying - Our dreams, our visions, our gifts, and our purpose. We do not recognize it because we make living our lives covered a "normal" part of our existence.

We tell ourselves that we are okay. We justify our covering by measuring ourselves by the other "covered" people around us. Yet, this covered life slowly drains the true life from us. It sabotages the very core of who we are.

It conceals our authenticity and sets us on a path to live our lies.

So, is this way of being, really okay? Is this the way you want to spend your days on this earth? Is this really how you want to occupy your time here? When you consider the life God intended you to have and the life you actually live, what conclusions do you draw? Are you truly content with where you are and the life you are living? Are you?

CHAPTER SIX:
I'm Not Who I am

I f you were to step outside of your life for a moment and become an observer, what would you see? What do you believe your life would show you? One thing is certain. Your life will show you how well or how poorly you have been living it. Your life will show you if you have been living it faithfully, truthfully...authentically.

How does your life show you these things? It shows you through opposites. Consider this. Deep down on the inside of you, underneath all of the leaves is the originally designed you. This is the place where all of your settings were initially established by your Creator, God. This is your core, the place of all things that were wonderfully made and strategically packaged, sealed, and branded inside of you. Your core houses your blueprint for authenticity. As such, your life shows you when you deviate from the detailed plans of the blueprint. When you are operating opposite to the established prototype, it shows – even if you are the only one seeing it.

You will see it when you stop feeling comfortable in the presence of the crowd that you once joined leaves with and shared mutual coverings. You will see it when you feel that tug in your soul or experience that feeling in your gut that something inside of you is not quite right. While you may not be able to identify exactly what it is, yet you know that it is something different – very, very different.

This dear friend is your authenticity calling out to you. It is calling your name as it makes its way through the jungle of leaves that have covered its path. It is aggressively pursuing you. Like a hunter lurking after its catch, it shadows you. Tracking your every move, it is waiting in the wings for an opportunity, just one opportunity to fulfill its mission – to address your secrets, expose your private lies, and to return you back to the blueprint plans of your existence. The question is, are you willing to be captured? Are you willing to allow authenticity to consume your life? Are you willing to surrender? Your life is calling to you. Are you listening?

What Is Life Saying?

Our life is always speaking to us. All around us, in every turn, with each step, we will find the voice of our life. We can hear it in everything we do. Our life speaks and echoes from every decision and choice we make. Our life speaks through our conversations and through every word we utter. Our life speaks through the ways in which we think. Our life speaks in our behavior and our actions.

Our life is also speaking each morning if we are waking up with dread, anxiety and a host of other counterproductive thoughts or feelings that keep us confused and overwhelmed. Our life is speaking when the thought of stepping out of bed brings a quiet dismay that causes us to silently wish the night was longer. It is speaking when neither God nor his plan prompts excitement; rather the thought of either reminds us of just how far away we feel from him.

Most importantly, and of greatest relevancy to this book, is the fact that our life is speaking to us each time we make the choice to cover, hide, or deny the real us that screams to be released from the layers of covering that have tried to keep it silent for far too long. Our life is speaking – it is speaking not from outside of us, but rather it is speaking from within us.

When our life speaks, it is the measure by which we can readily determine if we are living a life of truth or if we are living a life of consequences. When our life speaks to us, its voice is loaded with information we need for self-assessment, for discernment, for reflection, for correction, and for change. When our lives speak to us, its messages carry everything we need in our pursuit of authenticity. Our lives tell us the truth about who we are, where we are, and what we are. Our lives and the way we live them on a day-to-day basis do not lie to us. Our lives are always speaking. Our lives are always awaiting our response. What is your life speaking? Are you listening?

Like The Woman...

My Mouth

In Genesis 3:2-3, then the woman opens her mouth to speak to the serpent, *"Of course we may eat fruit from the trees in the garden,"* the woman replied. *It's only the fruit from the tree in the middle of the garden that we are not allowed eat. God said, 'You must not eat it or even touch it; if you do, you will die'"* (NLT).

This is where the conversation began. I remember the first time I read the third chapter of Genesis, the first question that came to mind was, why did the woman find it necessary to have a conversation with the serpent? Why?! At first glance, it seems ludicrous that any woman in her right mind would be entertaining a conversation with a snake. I know for sure if any creature – any one of them, on the face of the earth, spoke one word to me – just one – the remaining words it tried to speak to me would be behind my back as I am running away. You get the picture?

However, in all fairness to the woman, I believe when she opened her mouth to speak back to the serpent, she was doing so in an effort to provide information. In other words, this entire encounter began very innocently – at least on her part. The woman opened her mouth to say what God had said. She opened her mouth to explain. However, in her attempt to explain, she became vulnerable. She entered into dialogue with the one whose aim was to twist the very words she spoke and to attempt to use them for her destruction.

My own life grew darker from the enticement of entertaining conversations facilitated by the enemy of my soul. My conversations were with creatures that could not be seen by the naked eye because they existed in the spirit realm while hiding themselves behind the smiles of humans.

I am sure you have had the same types of conversations. At first, these conversations seem completely innocent. Like the woman, you are speaking the truth as you have known and believed it. You are speaking what God has spoken to you. You are giving the enemy insight as God has given it to you. You are informing him of the directives God has given you. You are letting him in on God's plan for your life. You are helping him see God's intention for your life. You are offering the promised plan for your life. But what we fail to understand is that while we are having these conversations, we are also giving the enemy too much information.

Some of my darkest moments in time occurred as a consequence of what I spoke out of my mouth. In my excitement and zeal, I haphazardly entered into conversations with those who did not have my best interest in mind. I dialogued with those who only sought information for their own gain, ungodly motives, or selfish ambition. I entered into conversations with the purest intent to provide information, only to find that the recipients of what I provided were the least grateful, the most envious, and the ones that secretly hoped for my failure.

I entertained conversations with those I considered to be close to me, sharing what I perceived to be the purpose for my life, only to see the covert workings of their jealousy and competition. My good intentions became my source of hurt and left me spiraling in disappointment. But more importantly, these conversations weakened me and made me vulnerable to more of the same. Why? Because out of my wounds, I began a cycle of behavior to either try to prove something to the ones that I never should have entertained conversations with in the first place. Matthew 7:6 says, *Do not give dogs what is sacred; do not throw your pearls to pigs. If you do, they may trample them under their feet, and then turn and tear you to pieces* (NIV).

Our unwise conversation can be the channel by which we give away our power – the intrinsic power that is ours by virtue of the fact we were created by a powerful God. It is these conversations that get us into the most horrible trouble. When we speak, how we speak, what we speak, and to whom we speak becomes the catalyst for a downward trajectory in our lives. It is not always the "bad" things we speak; in actuality it can be the things we speak while lacking understanding of the spiritual implications of our words.

Proverbs 18:21 says, *Death and life are in the power of the tongue, and those who love it will eat its fruit.* We can bring upon ourselves our own spiritual death when we open our mouths without wisdom, without discretion and without discernment. As a result, we become partakers of the *fruit* our words yield – the same fruit (metaphorically speaking) that existed in the middle of the Garden of Eden – the same fruit which God told the man and the woman they should not eat – the same fruit that once consumed, would bring about their certain death.

Like the woman, lacking good judgment in my conversations, I gave myself away into the hands of the one who wholeheartedly thirsted after my demise. And once in conversation, I became a target for the next level of his deception and disillusionment.

What we speak, how we speak, when we speak and with whom we speak can be the weapon we use to commit our own spiritual suicide.

WHO TOLD YOU THAT
YOU WERE NAKED?

So here you are. You are at a point of no return. If you have listened to your life – really listened, at this point you know too much to turn around now. Or at least you know if you turn around, there will be no peace on your journey. So where do you go from here? Go back! Yes, that is right. Go back! I know that we have been programmed to not visit our past and not rehash our experiences. But, in this instance I am extending you an invitation to go back so that you can go get your soul and allow it to catch up with what your life is telling you on this journey. Listen to your life right now. What is it telling you? Write down what you hear. How will you respond?

Reflection

_____

_____

_____

_____

_____

_____

_____

_____

_____

_____

_____

_____

_____

_____

_____

_____

PART THREE:

"What Is This You Have Done?"

Before We Start…

But what keeps us from telling ourselves the truth? What holds us back from our own personal interrogation and authentic response? The answer is…lack of intimacy.

I have been having some very serious conversations with God lately. Not that I didn't always take my conversations with him seriously – but I find myself in a very different place with him. My mind is different, my will is different, my emotions are different, and my very heart is different.

There is a deeper sense of longing for His presence, yearning for his touch, thirsting for his filling. I find myself in need of him…like the air I breathe, like the beat of my heart, like the blood that flows through my veins. I find that my utmost desire is to give myself to him and to receive him in return.

I literally have come to a profound place of total surrender. So, when I talk to him, it is from a sweet place of intimacy – a place that only the two of us can dwell and commune together. It's a quiet and secret place. It's a private get-a-way where the cares of this world are left at the door before I enter in with him. It's a place that continues to beckon me in the night and causes me to rise early in the morning. It's our place…mine and his.

It is here where he listens intently to my whispers, he inclines his ears to my call, and he draws near to me just because I'm there. It is here where I can hear his voice, I can feel his embrace, and I can consume his love.

Our place is one that the world can't penetrate, my enemies can't manipulate, and one in which Satan can't operate. It's our place...mine and his...our Intimacy!

CHAPTER SEVEN:
Seeing Blindly

When I was in the darkest room of my life, I really could not see. There was an absence of light which prevented me from being able to pierce the darkness. It was strange to be living a life where my physical eyes were perfectly fine, but the eyes that were the internal windows to my soul had been struck by blindness. I was spiritually handicapped by my sightless life. Trying desperately to navigate through the waters of my own deception, I pretended to have vision. My eyes covered with scales, I used my energy feeling my way through life. My endless maze of dark deception had entrapped me and confined me to a silent prison – a prison for which I held the key. But, the room was too dark and I was too blind to see that the key was in my hand.

Afraid of exposure, I did not allow myself to visit the prison harnessing my soul. I did not let others visit either. I allowed its existence to become my personal Alcatraz Island, my personal fortification, and stronghold. Therefore, I piled on layers and layers of leaves to keep others from recognizing my inadequacies. I assumed that if I covered them well enough, they would never be found and I could live my life happily ever after or at least convince others that I was living that way. After all, that was the thing that was most important to me – convincing others. However, the irony of my efforts was that in trying to fool the masses, I was the one being fooled.

Therefore, in these dark times of mine, I could not see my worth – not just my worth to God, but I could not see my worth to the world to which He had sent me to contribute. I had no clear understanding of my usefulness and purpose in the earth. The darkness prohibited me from seeing my value – my intrinsic excellence. The darkness caused me to lose sight of my importance and relevance to God's Kingdom. The darkness enveloping my soul dulled my view, and robbed me of genuine spiritual insight. I was lost – completely lost in the darkness. The greatest tragedy in this state of darkness is that I was hidden from the truth – my own truth – the truth of who God had created me to be. It was also here in this dark place that my life was speaking very loudly to me - very, very loudly.

Please Don't Look

As I lingered in my blinded stupor, another phenomenon was taking place in my life. The darker things became, I felt farther away from God. Yes, I knew he was there - somewhere in the distance. Yet, I did not feel close to him and I believed he had no desire to be close to me. How could he want to be close to me? I was disconnected. We seldom talked - not because I did not want to, but because I really did not have the words to explain where I was, what I was doing, and why I was doing it. I just did not have words. I did not know how to explain my fumbling clumsiness. I did not know how to tell him why I was stumbling, knocking things over, and breaking things. So, I preferred not to talk to him and I especially did not want him to talk to me. I suppose, I was hoping that he was also blind. I was hoping he could not see all I was working so hard to keep hidden from him.

But after all, that is what this type of blindness does. It robs us. It throws us off balance. It causes us to slip. It causes us to fall. It renders us incompetent. Yet, what is most amazing is that while we know we are blind and that we have these issues, we try to keep it hidden, while attempting to convince or rather fool others that we can see just fine. We become completely functional in our dysfunction, so much so that our dysfunction becomes our norm.

Here is a NEWSFLASH: No matter how much we try to hide our blindness, others around us can clearly see that we have no sight. While they may have never spoken this truth to us, they have certainly experienced the impact of our impairment. They have felt us bump into them. They have watched us stumble over them. They have witnessed us step on them. When we are blind, it impacts others around us. Perhaps, we hope they will not notice.

CHAPTER EIGHT:
Did You Hear Anything I Said?

"Then the LORD God said to the woman, 'What is this you have done?'" (Genesis 3:13). What God was really asking was, who or what have you allowed to influence your choices? Who or what have you allowed to cause you to deviate from my plan for your life? To what have you been exposed? Why did you let go of my promise, my word, and my intent for your life? What was the woman's response? The same as the Man's – Blame! "The serpent deceived me, and I ate" (Genesis 13:13). However, both the Man and the Woman totally missed the magnitude of God's questions.

The Man and the Woman missed the fact that God's questions were not about why they hid, nor was it about identifying a co-conspirator involved in the act of eating the fruit. The questions were about helping them:

1.) to recognize that what they thought they were hiding, they really were not hiding at all.

2.) to see how their actions had now caused them to become misplaced in the purpose and plan for which they were created

3.) to understand that because they listened to external sources, they had now traded in the truth for a lie that would open the door to the vulnerability to living life covered.

Furthermore, the Woman missed the fact that God's question was not about what she had done in the moment. The question was not about the fact that she had a conversation with the serpent. The question was not even about the fact that she offered some of what she was eating to the Man. The question, "What have you done?" was about getting the woman:

1.) to recognize that she had been convinced to step away from God's prescribed plan for her life.

2.) to realize the damage of her choice.

3.) to understand that her acquiescence to Satan would now open the door to greater vulnerability to his deception and lies.

4.) to see that she had traded in her God-given influence and power in one conversation that was simply wrapped in the appeal of instant gratification.

Both the Man and the Woman had been deceived and their deception became the very first garment they ever wore. And so it is with us.

Time and time again we have repeated the history of the Man and the Woman in our own lives. We have listened to the wrong voices. We have been influenced by the wrong sources. We have been deceived by a notion that seemed better than the truth. And like the Man and the Woman, in these instances of gross misalignment in our lives, instead of running to God, we learned to run away from God. We learned to hide. We learned to create disguises that would conceal the secrets of our actions. But, what we fail to realize is that a secret is not a secret to a God who knows all – and to a God that never called us to live undercover.

Like The Woman...

My Eyes

After the woman opened her ears to the voice of the serpent and after she spoke with him in conversation, she gave him space to deceive her through her eyes. In verses 4-5 the serpent speaks back to the woman, *"You won't die!" the serpent replied to the woman. God knows that your eyes will be opened as soon as you eat it and you will be like God, knowing both good and evil." The woman was convinced. She saw that the tree was beautiful and its fruit looked delicious, and she wanted the wisdom it would give her* (NLT).

It has been said that, "The eyes are the windows to the soul" (Cicero). If that is true, the woman gave complete consent for the enemy to access her windows, crawl inside and wreak havoc on the core of who God had been created to be. Taking her eyes off of all she had and falling for the unseen limitations of what she was being offered, she became the victim of wicked and vicious deception.

In the midst of my own deception, I gave the enemy space in my life. Yes, my eyes were opened, but opened to the darkness. My pursuit of the illusion of "beautiful fruit" and the wisdom and knowledge it would bring only led me deeper into the darkness. You see, we can never step away from the plan and purpose of God and still have light. When we deviate from His will and expect wisdom to be our guide, any semblance of light is removed from our path. Yet, when the true light is gone, we try to manufacture light for ourselves. We step into the role of God, trying to illuminate our path with people, places, and things – anything that will give us flash, sparkle, and shine. We turn our eyes toward striving in life. Accomplishment becomes our goal. Competition becomes our driving force. Winning becomes our passion. "One upping" the next person becomes our satisfaction. Manipulation becomes our mode of operation. We thrive on "connecting" ourselves with the right people, "networking" in the right circles, and "advancing" our personal agendas in an effort to get ourselves to the next level.

All this happens, simply because we moved our eyes. It is here where we literally lose our focus. It is here where we forget the promises and the plan of God. It is here where we begin to believe that our life is our own and that we can do with it what we please. It is here that we believe that we control our fate. It is here that we no longer remember all that has been created in us and for us. It is here in the heat of deception that we forget. There is nothing more tragic than believing we are seeing, when in actuality we are walking in total and complete darkness and utterly void of a clear understanding of who we are, our own worth, our own value and any real sense of authenticity.

WHAT IS THIS YOU HAVE DONE?

In repeating the actions of the woman, I allowed the effects of darkness to be perpetuated in my life, over and over again. Dare to visit your dark places. Check the portals that ushered you into that place – your ears, your mouth, and your eyes. What caused you to go there? Who or what did you listen to? With who did you have conversations which influenced your path toward darkness? What caused your vision to shift to the extent that you took your eyes off God and placed them on other things? Listen to your life right now. What is it telling you? Write down what you hear. How will you respond?

Reflection

PART FOUR:

Freedom

Let's Pause Here for a Moment...

N ow that you have made it through the first three parts of this book, it is my hope that you have come face-to-face with yourself and with God. It is my hope that you have encountered him like never before. I hope that you have had moments of brutal honesty and instances of Divine revelation. It is my hope that you have made some powerfully amazing discoveries as a result of listening to your life. While I am sure that what you have discovered was not all "good stuff", it is the stuff that if responded to appropriately, will lead you to a good life – a very good life – the one created specifically for you and written in God's plans as a part of your original design.

It is also my hope that at this point you are earnestly examining where you have been and assessing every aspect of your life to determine if you have a true desire to live your life differently – if you have the courage to step away from the old and into the new – if you are willing to take the risk and all that comes with it…to be you – the real YOU. It is my hope that you are motivated to use the "bad stuff and the downright ugly stuff" as a catalyst for change. It is my hope that by now you have come face-to-face with your internal "Dr. Jekyll and Mr.

Hyde". It is my hope that you have come to recognize that there is so much more to your life and of your life than the one you have been living. It is my hope that you are ready to go deeper, much, much, deeper in search of your authentic identity.

Most importantly, it is my hope that you have come to recognize the critical importance of living your truth. I hope you have seen the necessity of walking in the uniqueness of who God created you to be. I hope you have heard his call to authenticity. I hope you are ready to uncover, to live naked, and to be free.

Join me in the next few chapters as I highlight the stories of four phenomenal women. These women were just like you. These women were just like me. These women were just like us - Covered. However, they longed deeply for what they knew was missing in their lives - Freedom. Walk with them as they share their journey from Counterfeit to Truth...

CHAPTER NINE:
"Removing the Gauze"
(by Naomi Washington)

I was the person that was always planning to celebrate everyone else, making sure that others were OK when difficulties arose and lending the hand that she did not have in order to help someone out with a situation. I was the person who took care of everyone else. I did all these things to no avail.

I came from a family of mothers, teachers, nurses, sisters and aunts who took care of all those who were in arms reach and all those who needed the reach to be extended. At the end of each day the focus and goal was to make sure nothing was left undone.

It began as a child. I did what I was told and even what was suggested to make everyone around me happy and pleased with me. I held on to the theory of going to college made you a great person and getting a master's degree made you even better. I understood that being a great wife meant cooking every day and making sure your home was clean. I knew that the perfect Christian was in school every Sunday. I had accepted that there were standards on my job that made you professional and stand out and I strived to do all these things at once. I had done everything that others felt was pleasing and even assumed would make me successful in their eyes. When others became disappointed in me I felt like a failure.

When it was suggested to me that I should do something and it was likely I would not be able to accomplish the task, I would internalize the devastation. It would lead me to frustration and an explosion of tears. I was supposed to live and have the perfect life acceptable to others. I know now that I was literally filling the passion, dreams and desires I had for my own life with the expectations and happiness of others. It was like I was filling a wound with gauze and never properly coming back to treat it.

I was becoming frustrated inside because I was not meeting the expectations of others, or at least I thought I was not meeting them. In reality, I was suffering exhaustion. I was exhausted with the requirements I was trying to sustain and understand all at the same time. I was no longer operating on normal functions. My entire body was running often times on adrenaline. I was tired, had headaches, and was not eating because I was not physically hungry. In 2009, all my internal frustrations were beginning to manifest in my physical body. For 6 months of that year, I lived out the hardest and most crucial moments I have ever experienced.

I was a married 27 year old who had just completed a Master's Degree program with a 1, 4 and 9 year old. My father was suffering from cancer and it was progressing faster than my knowledge and understanding of the disease could handle. I was still mending my relationship with him after I felt abandoned by him at some of the most crucial times in my life. It was in April of 2009 that I suffered a TIA (Transient Ischemic Attack) or Mini Stroke. Because I did not see myself as a priority, I delayed my follow-up appointment with the family doctor. I was silently suffering from headaches and nose bleeds because an aspirin a day was supposed to fix the issue.

When I finally went to the doctor in June, the doctor found a brain aneurysm. This aneurysm was located on the right side of my brain continuing to grow due to stress. I remember hearing the nurse say that one was found but I do not remember the rest of the conversation. My father died in July and the treatment for my aneurysm was completed at the end of the month. My nephew was born on Friday and I had a endovascular coiling on Monday morning. He and I were in separate hospitals but both in the intensive care unit.

It was in that year that I realized I was living my life cast in a supporting role for the life of everyone around me. I had completely vacated the leading role in my own life. Essentially, the credits were about to roll! I had to make some decisions. I had to live out the true meaning of who I was before I let the stress of responsibilities and roles destroy me.

I became determined after a few doctors' visits that I needed to make my own options. I still had work to do. I still had to make a decision about my life. In the ICU after my endovascular coiling, I made a decision. I finally decided that I had purpose. There was a reason that God allowed me to remain. I was 27 years old. I was so many things to so many people but to me I was just Naomi. I like to say, Jesus and I had a meeting. We decided that I was going to learn to live out my life with purpose. I was going to be true to my happiness and create a joy in my own spirit. I was going to make sure that when all else around me was falling, I would have something to hold on to with grip. I would hold on to him.

There has never been a medical explanation for what was manifested in my body and it has been monitored for the past five years with no signs of recurring. If I never have an elaborate explanation I am certain enough that God was calling me to be authentic about my purpose. He was calling me to be authentic about his desire and design for my life. It was time to remove the gauze and go to work on becoming the authentic Naomi I was destined to be.

Naomi P. Washington *is the author behind NewPlaceWithin. She candidly writes and speaks about the joys and challenges of life, relationships and the journey to self-awareness. She is dedicated to helping others personally and professionally with years of experience in social work. Her passion and commitment is to inspire, motivate and encourage others to walk into their Designed Destiny.*

CHAPTER TEN:

"Stepping Out of My Clothes"

(by Dr. Stephanie Kripa Cooper-Lewter)

Recently my beautiful early-morning walking friend Christine began a personal fitness training program with Jimmy, "The Fat Burning Coach." Christine inspired Katrina and I with her unwavering dedication to meal preparation and commitment to get fit through serious muscle-building workouts. Soon, Katrina moved forward on faith and joined Jimmy's program. As Katrina completed her personalized assessment process, she invited me to accompany her for the final task of taking a "before" picture prior to beginning her intense eating and workout regimen.

Katrina and I talked together on our drive to the fitness center declaring "before" pictures would never be shown to a single soul. After arriving, I patiently waited as Katrina completed her fitness consultation anxious to hear how it went. Once we got back to the car, Katrina expressively described the process of *stepping out of her clothes,* feeling vulnerable and exposed standing in a sports bra and shorts in front of others and a camera. As she continued to share, unexpected tears welled up in my eyes, surprising us both.

In my spiritual walk, I have learned tears are a signal to pause and pay attention; they are often God's quiet nudging at my soul. In that moment, my heart empathized with Katrina; I was awed by her courage. The thought of taking a "before" picture terrified me. I couldn't imagine having the inner strength to stand uncovered for a camera and in front of people you hardly know. For more than a decade I struggled with extra body weight despite a newfound love of running, coupled with multiple starts and stops at the gym. All too often, self-care fell last on my list of priorities as I balanced other important identities I cherish: daughter, sister, woman, wife, mother, friend and confidant.

As I paid attention to my tears, I discovered a profound awakening. My outer struggle with weight reflected some of the innermost, unspoken burdens of my heart. Starting from my beginnings, these burdens slowly accumulated over time and were buried beneath the weight of expectations others placed on me, along with my own. As a baby, I was placed in Mother Teresa's orphanage in India – left without a name, a family, an identity, or a home. Most likely, I was given away because I was a girl. Declared abandoned, I was selected for adoption to the United States of America thousands of miles away. As I left India, I lost something that many take for granted, a sense of identity that is grounded in knowing your beginning story, who you are connected to and the place where you are from. As a child, my heart didn't understand why my Indian mother would give me away; a baby girl that had done nothing wrong but show up in this world.

Messages of doubt began to seep into my soul: orphaned, unwanted, unlovable, not good enough, broken and alone. Without role models growing up that reflected Indian women's beauty, I felt ashamed of my brown-skinned Indian features. I also had two visible scars on my left thigh from my time in India. I cringed when asked questions about these scars. In essence, my body was a daily visible reminder of India, a place I no longer understood, my lost genetic heritage and biological connections. It was on this broken foundation that I began hiding *who I was* behind layers of clothes resulting in choices that confirmed I felt less than whole.

Our body is often the place we carry our deepest shame and secrets. We hold the weight of our toxic silence each time we ignore our inner voice, missing opportunities to process and heal. Like so many women I have counseled and coached, we often move through the motions of our lives holding unexpressed pain, guilt, grief and regret as we strive to reach an unattainable image of outer perfection. Our symptoms can range from weight gain, to eating disorders, shattered relationships, unplanned pregnancies, abortions, affairs, broken marriages, parenting struggles, and other heartaches.

We *bury*, we *stuff*, we *hide*, we *layer* to cover our shame and struggles. Eventually our bodies and souls grow weary. God's call to authenticity asks us to show up fully, imperfections and all, and say in brave spaces: "This is who I am in the moment and this is what I need on my path to wholeness." Reflecting on this spiritual lesson, I moved forward on faith and signed up for the personal training program, like Christine and Katrina. As I *stepped out of my clothes* for my "before" picture and fought to keep my tears from flowing, Jimmy gently reassured: "This is the old you. I see a stronger you and who you will become." It took courage to remove the layers of clothes I hid behind and allow some of my deepest insecurities to be in full view. I realized in that moment my clothes were a metaphor for the illusions I needed to let go of in order to reclaim my voice, body and freedom.

You are a beautiful creation in God's eyes. No matter your life circumstances, you are loved, you are worthy, you matter.

Identify self-defeating beliefs that hold you back and replace them with those that strengthen your heart, mind, body and soul. Claim the promise that you can be healthy and whole. Find brave spaces to share your innermost struggles with those who have earned your trust and the right to hear your story. Surround yourself with others on the journey to health and wellness; true friends will uplift, encourage and challenge you to grow. Pray for courage to step forward daily. Release the weight of unnecessary burdens. Replace shame with authenticity. Let your light shine fully. Your God-given potential, purpose and destiny waits, go ahead – *step out of your clothes.*

Stephanie Kripa Cooper-Lewter, *Ph.D., L.M.S.W., C.P.E.C. is a licensed master social worker, child welfare scholar, author, certified personal and executive coach. Dr. Stephanie Kripa Cooper-Lewter has extensive experience working in nonprofit, social service, health, educational, and philanthropic sectors, working with individuals and families. She received her Ph.D. from the University of South Carolina and is a graduate of the Coaching and Positive Psychology Institute.*

CHAPTER ELEVEN:

"Walking In Obedience"

(by Malai Pressley)

God has taught me that being transparent and living an open book life is what truly sets you free. Hiding the stories of our lives from others only pleases the enemy and not God. So with that said, here's my story.

I would love to say that I grew up in Charleston, SC enjoying its beautiful beaches and living a blissful life of obedience. However, that was not always the case for me as a child and even into young adulthood. At the age of three, my mother divorced after being in an extremely abusive relationship. She became a single mother, raising my younger brother and me alone with the help of my grandparents until I turned 8. At school I was the perfect angel. At home, I was a hard-headed little devil. I was often rebellious and lived by own my free will. At the age of 8, my mom got a boyfriend who began living with us. This situation started out well, but by the age of 11, her boyfriend was smoking marijuana and began using cocaine. Now that my mother's boyfriend knew he had her trust, he began sexually molesting me. This lasted for two years which caused me to become even more rebellious. We didn't attend church, but I knew there was a God. He would often reveal things to me in dreams. At the age of 13, I had a dream my mother's boyfriend had raped me which prompted me to tell her what was going on. She believed me and he left, but disobedience only perpetuated. At 14, I found out that the man who I thought was my biological dad was not my dad and it left me lost, confused, mad, and blaming my mother. Until this time, my mother, brother, and I were very close, but things changed and "I love you" and hugs were no longer a part of our interactions.

My life had become havocked with insecurity and my only focus was on self-preservation. I was sexually active by 16 and then it was time for college. While there, I was a great student academically, but socially I lived by the ways of the world by going out to clubs, drinking, and gossiping. It was my way of numbing the pains of life. A month after my college graduation, I found myself pregnant, getting married and finally going to church. During this time, I met my biological dad and things seemed to be going uphill. Although I was in the church, I wasn't *in* the church. I loved God, but wasn't *in* love with Him. I was still living like I wanted to and definitely not a life of obedience to God. The marriage was encompassed with adultery, arguing, excessive spending, and you name it.

In 2005, I was a divorced single mom of two children with no money and feeling hopeless. I had truly hit rock bottom. My life without God, a life of self-centeredness and self-preservation, had gotten me nowhere. This lasted for years until March 2009. While playing with my kids at a neighborhood playground, a man approached me and started talking to me about Christ and how he had changed his life. He told me about his life of drinking, doing drugs, and abusing women. I had heard testimonies at church, but none like his. It was real and unfiltered. I thought he was crazy, but I knew it was not a coincidence he was speaking to me that day. Now I know he was a vessel God had used to draw me closer to Him.

In the summer of 2009, I began attending church regularly and desiring to learn God's word. I started becoming more disciplined and self-controlled. At home, I would read the bible like it was the last thing on Earth. For me, it was my last thing and my last hope. I made it a daily routine to read my bible first thing in the morning, a devotional at lunch, and write in my prayer journal at night. My family and friends thought I had really lost it.

The Lord was softening my heart. One day I decided to sit down with my mom. We talked, cried, and said "I love you" after so many years. I called my brother to tell him "I love you" too. I also encouraged them to go read the bible and learn about how much God loves them. I would talk about Jesus to anyone who would listen. As I read God's word and surrounded myself with people who loved Him, my desires changed. God had changed my heart. He broke my heart for what broke His and crazy things started happening.

I had gotten a job teaching at the school where I had been substitute teaching and completed my student teaching. I started giving my money through tithing to church. For years, I would have nightmares about my mother's ex-boyfriend and what he did to me, but all of a sudden the nightmares were gone. I had forgiven him and now pray for him and other children who are and have been victims of childhood sexual abuse. My kids and I were praying at home and reading daily devotionals. I had forgiven my ex-husband for the things he did to hurt me in our divorce and I asked for his forgiveness in how I had hurt him in our marriage. I found myself not even wanting to listen to the same music. My kids and I looked forward to church on Sundays and still do.

Today, through God's grace and living in tune with the Holy Spirit I still live a life of obedience even in today's ever-changing world. Is it without challenges? Absolutely not. No day is the same. In being obedient, you have to be willing to pay a price. You will be judged, criticized, and at times persecuted for shining brightly for Christ - And often times by the people closest to you. Through obedience God has released many blessings into my life. He has sent me on a missions trip to the Philippines, a missions camp with our youth ministry a few years ago, had me lead a small group bible study, serve on the ministry team, and lead a women's center. He has blessed my children, my family, and my home. He has given me favor in my finances and in my calling as a teacher.

The Lord has completely changed my life and not to mention…tamed my tongue. He has brought me through so much and I know there is so much more He will bring me through. I once heard a pastor say, "God is determined to work with you so He can work through you." His word says that "He will never leave you nor forsake you" and I'm a living testimony.

For so long, I lived as a victim with many "shoulda, coulda, woulda's" in my life, but now I live victoriously saying "Lord have your way, I am child of the most High, I am His Princess". People always ask or wonder why I smile so much. I smile because I am happy. I smile because I am free of guilt and shame. I smile because I have been forgiven. I smile because I have forgiven. It's a smile of hope, joy, peace, and the greatest of all…love. Love for you and Jesus our Savior.

I hope that you will join me in living a life of obedience even when the world says it's all about self and live how you want. I also hope that I have encouraged you to share your story with others and love out loud for God.

Malai R. Pressley, Ed.S. is a native of Charleston, SC. She is an Educator in the public school system and also serves as Executive Director at The Center for Women at NorthStar. When she is not serving in the community, Malai enjoys spending time with her two children, Mari and Makhi.

CHAPTER TWELVE:

"Honored to Wear My Scars"

(As shared by Antoinette "Toni" Howell and
written by Katrina Spigner)

I met Toni when we ended up sitting next to each other on an airplane. Seated on row 28C, I had settled in for my flight and was checking email on my phone. Toni arrived at row 28 and informed me that she was seated next to me. I stood and stepped in the aisle to clear the way for her to take her seat. Once she moved in, I took my seat and resumed responding to email. However, as the plane continued to fill, another young lady stopped at row 28. But, instead of asking me to let her in so that she could take her seat, she asked me to slide over to the middle seat so that she could be closer to her boyfriend that was seated on the other side of the aisle on row 28.

Now, I must admit the first thought that went through my head was, "Absolutely not! You both should have planned better so that you could be seated together. I do not like sitting in the middle! That is why I selected the seat I wanted to sit in when I purchased my ticket!" However, before my internal tantrum could trickle down from my mind and escape through my mouth in the form of words, my heart kicked in and I just politely moved over to the middle seat so she could sit down. Once settled in, Toni leaned over and said to me, "That was a really nice thing you just did." I simply responded, "I did it for love." We both laughed as she stated, "Well, that is young love. Give them a few years and she would have been happy you were sitting between them!"

It was at this point, Toni and I struck up a conversation. We did the airplane small-talk: "Where are you from?" "Where are you going?" "Are you going for work or fun?" After the first two questions, Toni responded to the third by stating, "I have stage four breast cancer."

Toni went on to share that on September 4, 2013 the doctors told her that she was going to die within the next three months. She sat in disbelief and silence over the following moments as doctors reported that the breast cancer had spread to her lymph nodes and was already in multiple sites in her body. They further reported that the cancer was aggressive and could quickly move to her brain. In that instant, everything changed - because everything changes when you are being told you are going to die. With no other words left accept, "The devil is a liar!" - Toni began a journey she had never envisioned for her life.

Prior to this day, Toni had been focused on her work and *her* plans to accomplish the goals she had set for her on her perceived road to success. She was eating well, exercising, and doing all the things that people who value their health and well-being are supposed to do. She was living the life she planned and all was good in her world. But, now here she was facing a death sentence. Here she sat recognizing that things would never be the same again in her world. Cancer had interrupted *her* plans.

With everything shaken and rocked around her, Toni looked to the only One she knew had the power to bring her through. She turned faith and her trust to the God she knew loved her - the One that loved her when she did not love herself - the One that had not always been in the forefront of *her* plans, but the One she desperately needed now. She surrendered to her Father and her God.

As a result of her surrender, Toni found life and grace in coming to know how deeply God loved her. She found solace in the prayers of those who prayed for her from many different races, ethnicities, religions, reformations, and cultures and she believed. She believed that God would heal her and sustain her life. In faith, she believed the opposite of the doctors' reports. Never losing her faith, she simply believed. And in the process of believing, she learned these valuable lessons:

1. The journey was not been about cancer. It was about me really knowing and drawing closer to God.
2. Cancer was a small thing. There was a bigger picture in place for her life. God had bigger plans for her - bigger than she ever realized.
3. There is no love in this universe like the love of God.

So, Toni and I sat on the plane on August 30, 2014 and with one breast and no hair, Toni declared, "My God is AMAZING! He is just Amazing!" All I miss are my eyelashes because they kept things from getting in my eyes!"

Through periods of laughter and tears, Toni continued to testify of the goodness of God through this ordeal. She marveled at how good God had been to her. She reflected on the fact that her test results often confounded the doctors because they could not understand how she was still alive. Yet here we sat.

After rounds of radiation treatments and chemotherapy, the doctors inquired as to whether or not Toni waned to have reconstructive surgery for her breast. Without hesitation Toni declined, stating, "I don't need to reconstruct my breast. I am honored to wear these scars. They remind me of just how good God is – because I'm still here!"

Throughout this journey, Toni has been cared for by her amazing sisters, Ty and Monica and many other family members and friends. Toni faces each day with thanksgiving, without fear and without shame. She finds the highest honor in telling others about the healing power of God while she work to leave a legacy where others will remember her passion and fervor in sharing the goodness of God with every person she encountered. Facing each new day as a victory, Toni quietly shared, "I still have aches and I still have pain, but I am free!"

Toni Howell *and her family live in Maryland and continue to proclaim how good God is to them. Toni's moments of sharing with me are merely a small portion of a much bigger story that is still being told.*

CHAPTER THIRTEEN:
Your Freedom

As you read the powerful stories of these four amazing women, did you see glimpses of yourself in their struggles, in their trauma, and in their pain? As you paused to consider your own story did you see yourself in theirs? I ask because *these women are us and we are these women.* Their struggles have been our struggles. Their trauma has been our trauma. And, their pain has been our pain. Nevertheless, they have made the most important discovery we could ever make – Knowing and walking in truth makes us free!

Naomi found freedom as she removed the wrappings of the "Super Woman" mentality and believing that her existence on the planet was to save the world and all of the people in it. As a result of the impact of the huge misconception that we can be all things to all people, Naomi learned the truth that on the big stage of life, she is only called to play to an audience of One. People-pleasing has never been written in God's plan for our lives. Living to please those around us can wreck our bodies and our spirits and cause us to completely cover ourselves. We give up so much of who we are for the sake of others that we become hidden and unrecognizable. Most importantly, when we are consumed and covered with the burden of pleasing others, it prompts God to ask the question, "Where are you?"

Dr. Stephanie Kripa found freedom as she stepped away from beliefs and mindsets from her past that had covered her, held her hostage and kept her hidden. After tapping into the courage to face her struggles with not feeling she was enough, she found the strength to reach out to The God who is more than enough. It was here where she realized her beauty underneath the superficial. It was here where she learned that her past circumstances, her body image, nor her shame were elements which defined her. She came to recognize that she was defined by something much deeper than the natural eye could see. She heard the question ringing in her ear, "Who told you were naked?" Yet, the greater question was, "Why is your nakedness not okay?"

So, in her courageous step of faith, she grabbed and held onto God's definition of who she was. She finally understood that she was not defined by the world, but rather by her God-given inner beauty and her heart toward God. For each of us, this indeed, is the freedom that comes with our surrendered willingness to disrobe before God and to see our nakedness as a precious gift of authenticity.

Malai found freedom when she discovered the path that would lead her out of the residual effects of the devastating trauma she faced at an early age. As a result of a series of horrific events that lead to behaviors that caused her to spiral downward beyond anything she could have ever imagined; she realized the path she was on was swiftly leading to her ultimate destruction. She recognized that this was not her best life. This was not the life she wanted. This was not the life God wanted for her. She had not yet met her best self.

So, in the midst of her mess, she reached up from the rubble to grab the Hand of the only One that could lift and revive her. She committed to allowing God to lead her and she committed to following him. She walked away from the dreadful question, "What is this you have done?" and in to a life filled with "What are the things God has called me to do?"

Toni found freedom in the love of God. Through a change in her life's direction, she landed on a path that drew her closer to him. Although scarred, she found honor. Although shaken, she found stability. Although faced with death, she found life.

I am certainly not saying that our stories are exactly like the stories of these women. What I am saying is that we have all grappled with behaviors, attitudes, mindsets, beliefs, challenges, and lies that have shown up in our lives for the purpose of robbing us of our authenticity. Like the conversation in the garden, the intent has been to keep us from God's best for our lives – far away from his very best.

But here is the thing, just like God brought these four women to a place of freedom; he desires your freedom as well. The truth of the matter is – God loves you. I know that sounds very simple and that you can find the "God Loves You" message on bumper stickers, church signs, and t-shirts. You can find it Sunday school lessons, in Sunday morning sermons, in pamphlets about salvation, and even in the stories of these women.

But, I am asking you to stop right now and consider God's love for you as a part of your own life's story. God is and has always been present with you in every chapter and on every line. Perhaps you have not always seen him there. Thick layers and manufactured facades make it difficult to sense his presence and his closeness to us. But his love remains.

It is that love that beckons you. It is that love that speaks to your innermost being in soft whispers that call you to be vulnerable, to be transparent, and willing to allow unhealthy parts of you to die so that the original plan and intent for your life can live.

Consider these points again...

When you were born, you entered the earth with an assignment that was already pre-planned and established. It was an assignment only you could complete. You were sent here with a purpose for your existence – fully equipped with everything you would ever need to operate according to God's plan.

Ephesians 1:4 states, *Long before he laid down earth's foundations, he had us in mind.* You did not arrive on the scene as an afterthought; you were a "forethought." God did not think of you after he formed the world and then tried to figure out where to place you in it. He thought of you before he ever formed to world with a specific plan for your part in it. Therefore, because he preconceived your place in the world, he fashioned a unique plan filled with specificities for your design. He knew how he wanted to use you. He knew ways in which you would need to function in order to produce the end result he desired. He knew your strengths and your weaknesses. He knew, even while you only existed as a thought in his mind – he knew.

So with great focus and love, he foresaw and planned every single thing you would need in order to be successful in this world. He planned how you would be packaged and fully loaded to accomplish the tasks that would be yours during your stay on earth. In the sovereignty of his mind, he saw your days – every one of them, so that he might fashion you to withstand whatever those days would bring. Before the beginning of time, you were on the mind of God, still uncreated, but yet already a part of his creation.

The challenge we often face is that we do not truly understand who and what God has created us to be. We have not considered that there is a unique purpose and plan connected to our lives. We have not fully recognized that we are here on assignment and that our mission is to actively live that assignment. Many of us have lived the majority of our lives not knowing this truth or knowing it in a very superficial or artificial way. Religion or "church" often teaches us to pretend to know while in reality we are living with the lack of a deeper truth of who we really are. When the truth that we do not know begins to surface, we overwork to suppress it because it would mean that someone would recognize our inadequacies and most importantly, it means that we might see those inadequacies in ourselves. Therefore, we avoid the face-to-face encounters with ourselves and with our truth.

But, how would our lives really be different if we had the opportunity to meet and get to know the real us? How might our very own truth...make us free?

Finally...

It is my hope that you have felt his call to you as you have walked through the pages of this book. Yes, I did say I hope you *felt* his call. Deep down in the secret places of your existence, I hope you invited God in and I hope you felt him occupying the space you opened to him.

It is my hope that you gained a deeper knowledge of the God who loves you more than can be written in a sentence, a paragraph, or a book. I hope you realized his desire for you to live a life of deep truth and profound authenticity. It is my hope that you took the time to dig deeply - really deeply; to unearth those buried parts of yourself that you allowed to be covered with layer upon layer of life's happenings.

It is my hope that you addressed the issues in your mind, your will, and your emotions that have kept you thinking - believing that your life could be nothing more than an artificial representation of who you were originally created to be. I hope you committed to answering for yourself the critical questions posed in the first three sections of this book. It is my hope that you gave up holding on to a counterfeit life that had been taking "real life" out of you.

I hope you committed to a deeper love of yourself. I hope you embraced your imperfections, your scars, your hurt, your guilt, your shame, your limitations, and your shortcomings - recognizing that all of these things are a part of your story. They are a part of the experiences that have fashioned you into the beautifully created being you are. I hope you peeled back the layers of a lifestyle that has been less than God's best, to discover that he has so much more to offer you.

It is my hope that you gave yourself permission to let go. I hope that you found the courage to release artificiality and sabotaging behaviors, attitudes, and patterns. I hope you resolved to give up control of the uncontrollable and to find peace in the unchangeable. I hope you stepped out of your fears, away from your trepidation, and through your struggles in effort to emerge as a different you.

Finally, it is my sincere hope that you were transformed. I hope that you were renewed. I hope you committed to living the truth. I hope you started the pursuit of authenticity. I hope embraced your nakedness. I hope you were made free.

Reflection

CONCLUSION

...And Into The Light

Using the energy I had left; I lifted myself from the floor. With my bed serving as an altar to catch me, I fell forward on it and wept. I cried and I cried and I cried and I cried. Pouring from my soul were tears of sorrow, tears of hurt, tears of torment, tears of shame, tears of sadness, and tears of grief. Flowing like the water from an uncapped fire hydrant and bathing me in the process, my tears represented a multitude of emotions. My tears represented my struggle with living a dualistic life. My tears represented the fatigue of trying to hold it all together when everything in me had been falling apart. My tears represented the choices I had made - the ones that had brought me to the point of death. But most importantly, my tears represented life, or rather, the celebration of a life that had not ended. My tears, these tears, represented the fact that I was still here. I was still alive.

In that instant, it was overwhelmingly clear that God wanted me. He came looking for me. He had ordained a very different purpose for my existence, so this was the beginning of his process of uncovering me. Through a mind-boggling turn of events, he brought me face-to-face with his truth regarding his love for me. Through a very personal intervention with him, he snatched me out of the pit with the Strong Arm of his grace.

Over time, he lovingly peeled back my layers and helped me see - really see that my nakedness was his plan for my life. He helped me see that my coverings were killing me and that my shame was his opportunity. He loved me back to life through the truth I found. He loved me back to life, while healing my heart and sealing me in the truth and freedom that was mine to have from the very beginning. And now...I live naked and unashamed.

THE AUTHOR

Captivating. Passionate. Inspiring. These are just a few words that have been used to describe Katrina Spigner. An Author, Speaker, and Certified Personal & Executive Coach, Katrina Spigner writes for, speaks to, and coaches those seeking a purposeful path that leads to living a more authentic and fulfilling life. Through the good, the bad, and the ugly of her own life, Katrina has learned some powerful lessons which she candidly weaves into her writing, speaking, and coaching. Katrina is deeply committed to helping people thrive no matter the challenge.

Katrina is the author of this and two other books, *This Is for You!: 31 Days of Life-Changing Discoveries* (2008), *G.I.F.T.: Growing In Faith Today!* (2010).

As a speaker, trainer, and workshop facilitator, Katrina speaks for and conducts workshops at events and conferences for numerous organizations.

As a personal and executive coach, Katrina helps women reinvigorate their lives with new energy for passionate, purposeful, and powerful living.

As an entrepreneur, Katrina is the founder and CEO of Re-Source Solutions, LLC, a personal and professional growth and development company dedicated to providing "Real Answers, for Real People, with Real Questions." Founded by Katrina in 2007, Re-Source Solutions, LLC serves as the umbrella company for Katrina N.O.W., Solutions N.O.W., and breathe N.O.W Publishers which houses all products and services provided by Katrina. These products and services include but are not limited to, books, journals, CDs, media contributions, keynote presentations, workshops, retreats, and personal & executive coaching.

Katrina is a media contributor and has also been featured in and written articles for numerous magazines. Katrina has been a guest on a number of television and radio programs.

Katrina earned a Bachelor of Arts degree and a Masters degree in Social Work. She also earned a certificate in Clinical Pastoral Education. Additionally, Katrina earned her Certification in Personal & Executive Coaching from the Coaching and Positive Psychology Institute (CaPP). Katrina will complete her Doctor of Education in Organizational Leadership degree from Northeastern University in Boston, MA in 2016. Katrina is the proud mother of two beautiful children, a daugther-in-love, and two amazing grandsons who continue to motivate her on her journey.

WORKS CONSULTED

The American Heritage® Dictionary of the English Language, Fourth Edition copyright ©2000 by Houghton Mifflin Company. Updated in 2009. Published by Houghton Mifflin Company. All rights reserved.

ACKNOWLEDGEMENTS

To my Heavenly Father, thank you for uncovering me. To my mother, Ollie, the most loving caregiver of our family – for walking with me and supporting me through every challenge and cheering for me in every victory – Thank you for your constant and unconditional love. To Jamil, my amazing son and phenomenal man – I could not be more proud of the wonderful person you have become and the contributions you still have yet to give to the world – I am grateful that I get to receive them daily – thank you. To Kayla, my precious daughter – I stand in awe of your resilience and your authenticity. Your testimony and ministry to others will change lives in a very powerful way – just like it has already changed mine. To Jeremiah and Jacob, my wonderful grandsons - what amazing gifts you are. I could fill pages expressing my love and gratitude for you, but I will not. Just know that I hold it all in my heart. To Lolita, the newest addition to our family and what a lovely addition you are - I am grateful to God for joining your heart with Jamil's and adding you as my daughter-in-love! Kimberly and Kristie, my "favorite" sisters – For tag-teaming with me during the most horrific wrestling matches of my life. I am grateful that God made us sisters, but I am even more grateful that he made us friends. To my brother from another mother, Elijah John Huston, thank you for being a "Big Brother" to me – Your support and love have been invaluable to me all these years. From me to you – "I love you more than you love yourself." To Naomi Washington, Dr. Stephanie Cooper-Lewter, Malai Pressley, and Antoinette "Toni" Howell - thank you for sharing your powerful stories of transformation and freedom. You each offer tremendous gifts to the world – keep shining! To Pastor Brian and Susan Thomas - Thank you for praying for me and loving me as I healed. Your support and leadership are priceless. Finally, to Goodness and Mercy – my entourage, thank you for following me "all the days of my life" (Psalm 23:6).

Contact Katrina Spigner
www.KatrinaNow.com
Facebook: www.facebook.com/katrinanow
Twitter: @KatrinaNOW

CPSIA information can be obtained
at www.ICGtesting.com
Printed in the USA
FFOW03n1152281014
8374FF

9 781600 472640